This book is to be returned on or
the last date stamped below

WITHDRAWN

Figures in a Landscape

Figures in a Landscape

Writing from South Africa

Anthony Adams and Ken Durham

CAMBRIDGE
UNIVERSITY PRESS

Published by the Press Syndicate of the University of Cambridge

The Pitt Building, Trumpington Street, Cambridge CB2 IRP

40 West 20th Street, New York, NY 10011-4211, USA

10 Stamford Road, Oakleigh, Melbourne 3166, Australia

First published 1995

Printed in Great Britain at the University Press, Cambridge

A catalogue record for this book is available from the British Library

Library of Congress cataloguing in publication data

Writing from South Africa / Anthony Adams and Ken Durham.

    p.   cm. – (Figures in a landscape)

1. South African literature (English) 2. South Africa – Literary collections.

I. Adams, Anthony. II. Durham, Ken. III. Series.

PR9364.9.W74   1994

820.8′0968 – dc20   94–24804   CIP

ISBN 0 521 43572 2 (paperback)

Contents

Acknowledgements

We are grateful to a number of colleagues for their help in the preparation of this book. In particular we would like to thank Professor Honey of the Osaka International University and Andre Lemmer of the University of Port Elizabeth for their helpful comments on the introduction, and Professor Witold Tulasiewicz of Wolfson College, Cambridge, and the University of Calgary for much advice especially on the language section. We are also grateful to Wendy Boddy for her assistance in proof reading and to Sheila Hakin, Librarian, University of Cambridge Department of Education, for bibliographical advice and assistance.

Thanks are due to the following for permission to reproduce illustrations: p.2 Alberto Venzago/Magnum, Gerald Cubitt; p.8 Orde Eliason/Link © ; p.16 Arthus-Bertrand/Ardea; p.24 Orde Eliason/Link © ; p.32 Orde Eliason/ Link © ; p.40 Gerald Cubitt; p.48 Gideon Mendel/Network; p.60 © Chris Steele-Perkins/Magnum; p.82 Gideon Mendel/Network; p.94 Gerald Cubitt; p.104 Gerald Cubitt; p.120 Frank Spooner; p.129 Orde Eliason/Link ©.

Thanks are due to the following for permission to reproduce stories: p.1 'Unto Dust' by Herman Charles Bosman, © Human & Rousseau (Pty) Ltd; p.7 'The Dignity of Begging' by Bloke Modisane, permission by Ingeborg Modisane; p.41 Estate of Alan Paton for 'A Drink in the Passage' from *Debbie Go Home* by Alan Paton, 1961, Jonathan Cape; p.49 'The Park' by James Matthews © James Matthews; p.81 'One Last Look at Paradise Road' by Gladys Thomas from *Sometimes When It Rains*, © Oosthuizen 1987 (Pandora Press); p.95 'Shadows' from *Small Circle of Beings* by Damon Galgut, Constable & Co. Ltd, 1988; p.103 'Head Work' by Abel Phelps © Abel Phelps; p.109 'The Visitor' from *What's Love Got To Do With It?* by Deena Padayachee, COSAW Publishing (Pty) Ltd, 1992; 'Some Other Elsewhere' by Merle Colborne © Merle Colborne from *New Hippogriff Writing*, 1990 ed. Macphail; p.119 'The Moment Before the Gun Went Off' from *Jump and Other Stories* by Nadine Gordimer, first published in Great Britain by Bloomsbury Publishing Ltd, 1991.

Every attempt has been made to locate copyright holders for all material in this book. We were unable to trace the copyright holders of the other stories and would be grateful for any information that would enable us to do so.

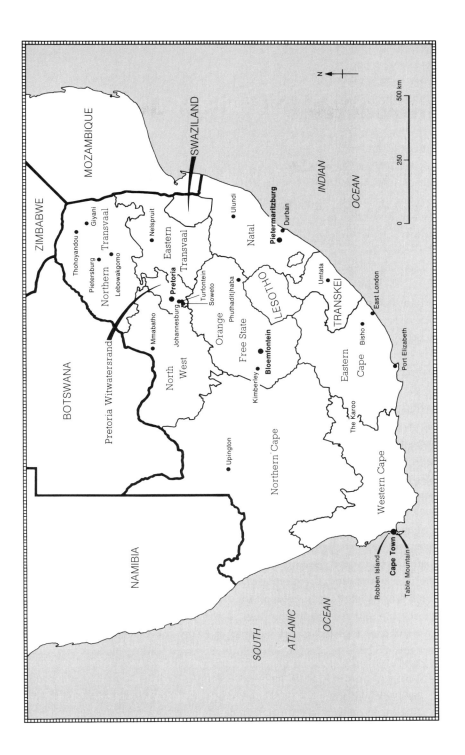

Introduction

The natural landscape of South Africa is extraordinarily varied and beautiful, ranging from the semi-desert highlands of the Karroo which cover nearly two-thirds of the country's interior to the majesty of Table Mountain and the beauty of the Cape in the south. By tradition, the original South African depended upon a rural economy. But, with the discovery by the European settlers of both diamonds and gold in the 1870s, large towns, such as Kimberley and Johannesburg, developed, and black African men became urbanised often having to leave their wives and families behind in the country while they went to work in the mines near the cities, frequently living in large hostels based upon tribal loyalties. Therefore the landscape of most of the stories in this collection is an urban one, echoing all the tensions and the struggles of the life of the towns in what is still a divided society.

With one exception, the tales in this collection are arranged in chronological order. The story of twentieth-century South Africa can be told in many ways, but it is important to realise that during much of the period covered by this collection, political power lay in the hands of the white National Party, dominated by White Afrikaners descended from Dutch settlers, who had arrived at the end of the seventeenth century. The Blacks, who, collectively, were numerically the largest group of peoples, were excluded from voting and forbidden to form political parties.

The National Party government was nothing if not paternalistic: it was common to hear Afrikaners describe the Blacks as 'children'. Part of their justification for the system was a belief that the Blacks were 'less developed' than the Whites and, therefore, needed protection for their own good. Under the Nationalist Party's rule in the 1950s and 1960s there was a rigid censorship and control of literature, with many books being banned by the government. This led to art being enlisted by the Blacks as part of their struggle against oppression. Thus Wally Serote, a leading Black writer, said:

> South African literature will not be judged by how writers chose words sensitively to say what they wanted to say . . . It will be judged by how it recorded and portrayed the struggle of our people for liberation, and by how much it contributes to the enhancement of a struggle.

The National Party consolidated and developed through legislation, after 1948, an already existing colour bar between White and Black into the system of 'apartheid' (the Afrikaans word literally means 'separateness') which divided the different races. This was given some semblance of respectability because it was a policy supported by the teaching of the Dutch Reformed Church, which indicated that the superior nature of the Whites over the Blacks was based upon the Scriptures and that it was God's intention that the white races should dominate the black ones. There were always some opponents amongst the Whites, including some Afrikaners, to this idea of 'separation', and a largely White-based Liberal Party emerged mainly to campaign against the programme of apartheid.

However, what first attracted most attention outside South Africa was the system of 'petty apartheid' which, for example, insisted upon separate entrances, benches and recreational areas, such as parks and beaches, for White and non-White people. James Matthews' story, 'The Park', well indicates the sense of being discriminated against which this system conveyed to many young non-White South Africans.

Much more seriously, however, the apartheid policies led to the system of classifying people into separate racial groups which included 'Whites' (often called 'Europeans', wherever they actually came from, so that at one stage Japanese were classified as 'honorary whites' so they could stay in hotels restricted to whites only), 'Blacks' (often called 'Africans' or, offensively, 'Bantus', divided into various ethnic groups, or tribes), 'Indians' (especially in Natal, where there was a large Indian population) and 'Coloureds' (those of mixed racial origin, often the offspring of a White 'master' and a Black 'servant'). The Whites tended to group themselves into the Afrikaners, who had developed their own language, known as Afrikaans, and other Whites, for example those who originally came from Britain or Ireland and who were called 'English speaking South Africans' (ESSAs).

Several of the authors represented here were at one time or another 'banned', their books forbidden to be on public sale or even read in libraries. Some of their stories were first published in a famous Black South African magazine, *Drum*, which (itself frequently banned) gave an opportunity for new young writers to find a voice and an audience. Not surprisingly, many of these writers (often in and out of prison) were very angry at the injustice of their society, which explains the violence in much of their writing. A more 'pleasant' collection would have been much less true to the times that they have experienced and describe. This collection of stories seeks to show how people struggle to survive against a further landscape, that of political turmoil and change.

The exception to the chronological arrangement, mentioned above, is Normavenda Mathiane's 'Labour Pains', which we have placed at the end because, in the moving picture it presents of a new land waiting to be born, it exactly captures the complex mood of uncertainty as well as hope and expectation experienced in South Africa since 1990, with the long-awaited release of Nelson Mandela from his many years of imprisonment on the impregnable natural fortress of Robben Island, off-shore from Cape Town. It is difficult to exaggerate the symbolic, as well as the practical political, importance of that moment.

Mandela had been President of the African National Congress (ANC) and had been imprisoned for so-called crimes against the state. This arose from the attempts of the ANC in 1955 to provide a blueprint – 'The Freedom Charter' – for a future South Africa that would no longer be dominated by the White Afrikaner National Party. The Charter, a widely accepted document amongst Blacks, was based upon Marxist principles, and its total rejection by the majority of the Whites led to the beginnings of the 'Armed Struggle', whereby the ANC tried to achieve its ends by urban-guerrilla tactics. This led to the imprisonment of Mandela (who supported the Armed Struggle) and the banning of the Communist Party and the ANC, although this did not prevent the ANC from continuing as a very powerful underground resistance movement. It is against this background that the impact of the release of Mandela and the 'unbanning' of the Communist Party and the ANC must be seen. Subsequently, the once-banned ANC has become a major negotiating body with the reformed National Party in evolving a constitution for the new South Africa. The efforts of these two parties to ensure the holding of a non-racially based General Election in April 1994 led to a regrouping of political forces, with the ANC and the National Party supporting free elections, opposed initially by the largely Zulu-based Inkatha Party and by the extreme right-wing Whites, both of which would like to see a federal South Africa where they could have separate 'states' of their own.

In 1952, the Pass Laws forced all 'Africans' to carry a 'reference book' (sometimes ironically called the 'Book of Life'): an identity document containing details of where they lived, their employment and a huge amount of other personal data. This had to be carried at all times and was a particularly hated symbol of an increasingly oppressive regime. In 1973 (18 January) the *Cape Times* reported:

> Chief Gatsha Buthelezi of KwaZulu yesterday denounced reference books as symbols of oppression and the greatest cause of resentment between Whites and Africans. Waving his own passbook in the air, the Chief reminded the special session of the KwaZulu Legislative Assembly . . . that he had been arrested several times for not carrying it.

If this could happen to so politically important a figure as Buthelezi (who emerged alongside Mandela to be one of the major Black leaders in South Africa, with his Inkatha Party an important rival to the ANC), it is easy to imagine the effect the Pass Laws had upon the population as a whole.

The system of classification by race and the Pass Laws paved the way for even more hated aspects of apartheid: the Group Areas Act, the Immorality Act and the 'Bantu' Education Act.

The first of these laid down in precise terms those places where 'Europeans' could live and those which were set aside for Africans or other racial groups. This meant, for example, that Africans would come to their daily work in Johannesburg every morning by over-crowded trains, used rather like cattle-trucks, from their home areas some miles outside the city – places such as the specially created 'township' of Soweto (an artificial name meaning 'South West Township'), which Whites were forbidden to enter without special permission. This had the effect of ensuring that many White South Africans, including some of the most liberal, often lived in considerable luxury, away from the realities of the squalor and poverty of those living in the townships. The stories in this collection contain frequent references to the townships (or 'locations' as they were often known) and the landscape of the South Africa of this time cannot possibly be understood without reference to this institutionalised division not only among races but also between rich and poor.

The Group Areas Act was a key plank in the policy of 'grand apartheid', or 'separate development', which was pursued from the time the National Party came to power in 1948 until 1990. This led to the setting up of separate tribal homelands, known as 'Bantustans'. These had their own supposedly independent governments, though they were puppet administrations, entirely dependent for economic and military support upon South Africa and not recognised as independent states by any other government in the world.

The racial divisions created by the policy of apartheid carried over into state control of people's personal and private lives, whatever their ethnic background. Thus, the so-called Immorality Act outlawed all sexual and many social relations between Blacks and Whites, which meant, of course, that there could be no legal marriages across the colour divide.

Finally, the 'Bantu' Education Act (misnamed since it identified all 'Africans' as 'Bantus' instead of recognising the distinctive nature of their different tribes) reinforced the already segregated school system by requiring that instruction of Africans in primary schools should be in their own mother-tongue, though this was not always put into practice. To those outside, this might almost have seemed a progressive measure but those Africans who did attend school (schooling being voluntary for them) wanted above all access to English, which they saw as a wider base for communication than their own tribal language, or Afrikaans, the language of the hated oppressors. Mutloatse's story, 'The Truth, Mama', shows some of the consequences for family life of a determination to fight against the implications of this Act, a determination which often led to young Blacks refusing to attend school, instead roaming the streets as beggars or in street-wise gangs of young criminals, known as 'tsotsis'.

In the 1980s, international opinion led to the rest of the world refusing to trade with South Africa and a consequent weakening of its economy. There was also an increased recourse to violent struggle by the ANC. Even the National Party came, under these pressures, to recognise that the cruel system of oppression could not be sustained for ever. Therefore all of these Acts, the very scaffolding of apartheid, were gradually dismantled, and most of the structure of 'petty apartheid' itself disappeared. The culmination of all this was the release of Mandela by the government in 1990.

Many of the stories in the first half of this collection relate to the period when all the aspects of apartheid were at their height, and the writers respond to them with a mixture of anger and bitter humour. In some ways such humour was the best response since the system of classification became so absurdly developed by the bureaucracy of government that only sardonic laughter could expose it for what it was.

There is a considerable change of tone in the stories in this collection, which justifies their chronological ordering. The opening story, 'Unto Dust' by Bosman, himself an Afrikaner and therefore betraying his own 'tribe' in writing as he does, powerfully exposes the absurdities of a system of government and social control built upon race. Bosman's inclusion in this collection is an important reminder that we must not make the same mistake as the Nationalist Government and stereotype people according to their racial origin. Some of the most outspoken opponents of the government, even in the worst days of apartheid, have been found amongst the Afrikaners themselves.

Those stories written at the height of the most troubled period, from the 1950s onwards until the 1980s, are, for the most part, bitter, angry and often violent. From the mid-1980s onwards, however, much South African writing takes on a new tone. You can almost sense that, as the apparatus of apartheid started to crumble, South African writers began to abandon social and political concerns and returned to the more mainstream literary themes of personal and family relationships. This can be seen in the work of Merle Colborne and Damon Galgut. Obviously, in many modern South African writers the political concerns and references are still there but, as changes take place and a more optimistic mood emerges, they are frequently treated differently. Abel Phelps is able to deal with the absurdities of the racial groupings with a humour that is quite different from the bitter irony of Bosman, thirty years earlier.

Reporting in the *Guardian* (9 January 1993) on a conference on the future of South African writing, James Wood suggested that 'South Africa's literature has been conquered by apartheid' and that the work of the conference was to try to 'free it'. He quotes J. M. Coetzee, one of the best-known novelists, as saying:

> South African literature is a literature in bondage . . . It is a less than fully human literature . . . It is exactly the kind of literature that you would expect people to write from a prison.

This may be true of some of the earlier stories represented here, though, even then, the most successful literary works skilfully entwine political and personal elements, seen for example in Bessie Head's 'The Prisoner Wore Glasses'. It is even more true of the work that can be seen in the new tradition that is beginning to develop. It is a fitting symbol of the changes that are taking place that the 1991 Nobel Prize for Literature should have gone to a woman South African writer, Nadine Gordimer, represented here by her story, 'The Moment Before the Gun Went Off'. Whilst this quite clearly derives from the bitter history of the events summarised in this introduction, the human qualities and heartaches of individuals living in that place and time are there also. It is in stories like these, that the South African literature of the later twentieth century is beginning to discover its new, distinctive and gentler voice.

Unto Dust

HERMAN CHARLES BOSMAN   1949

Bosman, born as long ago as 1905, near Cape Town of Afrikaner parents, is a uniquely powerful writer of satirical short stories. At the time he wrote this and many of his other stories it would require great courage for him as an Afrikaner to criticise the racist values of many of his fellow-countrymen. Here he points to the many absurdities of the doctrine of apartheid and celebrates the common humanity and mortality of both white man and kaffir — 'dead you had difficulty in telling them apart'. As so frequently in his work, Bosman tells his tale through the voice of a prejudiced story-teller whom he presents to us in an ironic manner.

I have noticed that when a young man or woman dies, people get the feeling that there is something beautiful and touching in the event, and that it is different from the death of an old person. In the thought, say, of a girl of twenty sinking into an untimely grave, there is a sweet wistfulness that makes people talk all kinds of romantic words. She died, they say, young, she that was so full of life and so fair. She was a flower that withered before it bloomed, they say, and it all seems so fitting and beautiful that there is a good deal of resentment, at the funeral, over the crude questions that a couple of men in plain clothes from the landdrost's office are asking about cattle-dip.

But when you have grown old, nobody is very much interested in the manner of your dying. Nobody except you yourself, that is. And I think that your past life has got a lot to do with the way you feel when you get near the end of your days. I remember how, when he was lying on his death-bed, Andries Wessels kept on telling us that it was because of the blameless path he had trodden from his earliest years that he could compose himself in peace to lay down his burdens. And I certainly never saw a man breathe his last more tranquilly, seeing that right up to the end he kept on murmuring to us how happy he was, with heavenly hosts and invisible choirs of angels all around him.

Just before he died, he told us that the angels had even become visible. They were medium-sized angels, he said, and they had cloven hoofs and carried

Monument to General Botha

forks. It was obvious that Andries Wessels's ideas were getting a bit confused by then, but all the same I never saw a man die in a more hallowed sort of calm.

Once, during the malaria season in the Eastern Transvaal, it seemed to me, when I was in a high fever and like to die, that the whole world was a big burial-ground. I thought it was the earth itself that was a graveyard, and not just those little fenced-in bits of land dotted with tombstones, in the shade of a Western Province oak tree or by the side of a Transvaal koppie. This was a nightmare that worried me a great deal, and so I was very glad, when I recovered from the fever, to think that we Boers had properly marked-out places on our farms for white people to be laid to rest in, in a civilised Christian way, instead of having to be buried just anyhow, along with a dead wild-cat, maybe, or a Bushman with a claypot, and things.

When I mentioned this to my friend, Stoffel Oosthuizen, who was in the Low Country with me at the time, he agreed with me wholeheartedly. There were people who talked in a high-flown way of death as the great leveller, he said, and those high-flown people also declared that everyone was made kin by death. He would still like to see those things proved, Stoffel Oosthuizen said. After all, that was one of the reasons why the Boers trekked away into the Transvaal and the Free State, he said, because the British Government wanted to give the vote to any Cape Coloured person walking about with a *kroes* head and big cracks in his feet.

The first time he heard that sort of talk about death coming to all of us alike, and making us all equal, Stoffel Oosthuizen's suspicions were aroused. It sounded like out of a speech made by one of those liberal Cape politicians, he explained.

I found something very comforting in Stoffel Oosthuizen's words.

Then, to illustrate his contention, Stoffel Oosthuizen told me a story of an incident that took place in a bygone Transvaal Kaffir War. I don't know whether he told the story incorrectly, or whether it was just that kind of story, but, by the time he had finished, all my uncertainties had, I discovered, come back to me.

'You can go and look at Hans Welman's tombstone any time you are at Nietverdiend,' Stoffel Oosthuizen said. 'The slab of red sandstone is weathered by now, of course, seeing how long ago it all happened. But the inscription is still legible. I was with Hans Welman on that morning when he fell. Our commando had been ambushed by the kaffirs and was retreating. I could do nothing for Hans Welman. Once, when I looked round, I saw a tall kaffir bending over him and plunging an assegai into him. Shortly afterwards I saw the kaffir stripping the clothes off Hans Welman. A yellow kaffir dog was yelping excitedly around his black master. Although I was in grave danger myself, with several dozen kaffirs making straight for me on foot through the bush, the fury I felt at the sight of what that tall kaffir was doing made me hazard a last shot. Reining in my horse, and taking what aim I could under the circumstances, I pressed the trigger. My luck was in. I saw the kaffir fall forward beside the naked body of Hans Welman. Then I set spurs to my horse and galloped off at full speed, with the foremost of my pursuers already almost upon me. The last I saw was that yellow dog bounding up to his master – whom I had wounded mortally, as we were to discover later.

'As you know, that kaffir war dragged on for a long time. There were few pitched battles. Mainly, what took place were bush skirmishes, like the one in which Hans Welman lost his life.

'After about six months, quiet of a sort was restored to the Marico and Zoutpansberg districts. Then the day came when I went out, in company of a handful of other burghers, to fetch in the remains of Hans Welman, at his widow's request, for burial in the little cemetery plot on the farm. We took a coffin with us on a Cape-cart.

'We located the scene of the skirmish without difficulty. Indeed, Hans Welman had been killed not very far from his own farm, which had been temporarily abandoned, together with the other farms in that part, during the time that the trouble with the kaffirs had lasted. We drove up to the spot where I remembered having seen Hans Welman lying dead on the ground, with the tall kaffir next to him. From a distance I again saw that yellow dog. He slipped away into the bush at our approach. I could not help feeling that there was something rather stirring about that beast's fidelity, even though it was bestowed on a dead kaffir.

'We were now confronted with a queer situation. We found that what was left of Hans Welman and the kaffir consisted of little more than pieces of sun-dried flesh and the dismembered fragments of bleached skeletons. The sun and wild animals and birds of prey had done their work. There was a heap of human bones, with here and there leathery strips of blackened flesh. But we could not tell which was the white man and which the kaffir. To make it still more confusing, a lot of bones were missing altogether, having no doubt been dragged away by wild animals into their lairs in the bush. Another thing was that Hans Welman and that kaffir had been just about the same size.'

Stoffel Oosthuizen paused in his narrative, and I let my imagination dwell for a moment on that situation. And I realised just how those Boers must have felt about it: about the thought of bringing the remains of a Transvaal burgher home to his widow for Christian burial, and perhaps having a lot of kaffir bones mixed up with the burgher – lying with him in the same tomb on which the mauve petals from the oleander overhead would fall.

'I remember one of our party saying that that was the worst of these kaffir wars,' Stoffel Oosthuizen continued. 'If it had been a war against the English, and part of a dead Englishman had got lifted into that coffin by mistake, it wouldn't have mattered so much,' he said.

There seemed to me in this story to be something as strange as the African veld. Stoffel Oosthuizen said that the little party of Boers spent almost a whole afternoon with the remains in order to try to get the white man sorted out from the kaffir. By the evening they had laid all they could find of what seemed like Hans Welman's bones in the coffin in the Cape-cart. The rest of the bones and flesh they buried on the spot.

Stoffel Oosthuizen added that, no matter what the difference in the colour of their skin had been, it was impossible to say that the kaffir's bones were less white than Hans Welman's. Nor was it possible to say that the kaffir's sun-dried flesh was any blacker than the white man's. Alive, you couldn't go wrong in distinguishing between a white man and a kaffir. Dead, you had great difficulty in telling them apart.

'Naturally, we burghers felt very bitter about this whole affair,' Stoffel Oosthuizen said, 'and our resentment was something that we couldn't explain, quite. Afterwards, several other men who were there that day told me that they had the same feelings of suppressed anger that I did. They wanted somebody – just once – to make a remark such as "in death they were not divided". Then you would have seen an outburst all right. Nobody did say anything like that, however. We all knew better. Two days later a funeral service was conducted in the little cemetery on the Welman farm, and shortly afterwards the sandstone memorial was erected that you can still see there.'

That was the story Stoffel Oosthuizen told me after I had recovered from the fever. It was a story that, as I have said, had in it features as strange as the

African veld. But it brought me no peace in my broodings after that attack of malaria. Especially when Stoffel Oosthuizen spoke of how he had occasion, one clear night when the stars shone, to pass that quiet graveyard on the Welman farm. Something leapt up from the mound beside the sandstone slab. It gave him quite a turn, Stoffel Oosthuizen said, for the third time – and in that way – to come across that yellow kaffir dog.

The Dignity of Begging

WILLIAM BLOKE MODISANE   1951

Modisane was born in the township of Sophiatown in 1923 where he lived until he left South Africa on an exit permit in 1951. He left school early, after his father had been murdered, and worked in a left-wing bookshop. He writes therefore with a full knowledge of the world that he describes – the world of the poor Black in towns such as Johannesburg, who often had no means of survival except by crime or begging. The hero of this story has turned begging into a profession – and done very well out of it. The tale is a half-comic account of a beggar-survivor and opposes the world of the city street which is his kingdom with the world of the rural environment which was his first home. It is a story filled with many contrasts – and some surprises.

The magistrate raises his eyes above the documents and plunges them like daggers into my heart. His blue eyes are shining with a brilliance that sets my heart pounding like the bass of a boogie-woogie.

'I'm sick to death of you . . . heartily sick. There is not a Native beggar on the streets whose full story I do not know,' the magistrate said. 'I have watched some of you grow up. There is not one I have not tried to rehabilitate many times. Some I was forced to send to gaol, but they always come back, they come back to the goose that lays the golden eggs.'

These are fighting words, the magistrate sounds as though he is going to put us away for a few weeks. My only regret is that Richard Serurubele has to share my fate. If only the magistrate knew that he is not a parasite like the rest of us, that he is what might be called an exploited beggar. He had been crippled by an automobile, and ever since then his parents have made capital out of it. They use him to beg so they can balance the family budget. They never show him the comfort of love. Relentlessly they drive him like an animal that has to work for its keep and feed. He is a 21-year-old lad who drags one foot along. He is an abject sight who has all the sadness of the world in his face; he looks many times older than my mother-in-law.

'You beggars make it difficult for me to do my duty. In spite of my constant failures to rehabilitate you, I always believe in giving you another chance . . . a

Rubber man, Johannesburg

fresh start you might call it,' the magistrate said. 'But I am almost certain that you'll be back here in a few days!'

The magistrate is getting soft, I can see my freedom at a distance of an arm's stretch, here is my chance to put on my act; a look of deep compassion and a few well-chosen words can do the trick. I clear my throat and squeeze a tear or two.

'Your Honour, most of us beg because we have been ostracised by our families; they treat us as though we were lepers,' I say, wiping off a tear. 'They want us to look up to them for all the things that we need, they never encourage us to earn our own keep. Nobody wants to employ us, people are more willing to offer us alms than give us jobs. All they do is show us pity. We don't want to be pitied, we want to be given a chance to prove that we are as good as anybody else.'

I can see from the silence in the court that everybody is deceived, the magistrate is as mute as the undertaker's parlour. I read pity spelled on the faces of all the people in the court; perhaps the most pathetic face is my own. I am magnificent, an answer to every film director's dream. I know that I have said enough – enough to let me out, that is. The magistrate looks at me compunctiously, I feel like jumping with joy and shouting hallelujah.

'I understand you are matriculated; Nathaniel is the name, isn't it?' he said, while turning a page of the report that was prepared by a worker of the Non-European Affairs Department. 'Yes, here we are, Nathaniel Mokmare. The department recommends that you be sent to a place where you will be taught some useful trade. I want you to report to Room 14 at the department's buildings tomorrow.'

This is not what I bargained for, my brilliant idea has boomeranged. Why must I take a job when I can earn twice a normal wage begging? After all, what will the horses do if I must take a job? I must uphold the dignity of begging. Whoever heard of a beggar working? It's unethical, that's all.

'As for you, Richard Serurubele, I'll let you go this time, but mark my words, the next time you appear before me, I will have to send you to the Bantu Refuge. Now get out of here, the both of you.'

If the magistrate had seen the big grin on my face as we left the court, he would have thrown my deformed carcass in gaol and deliberately lost the key. He does not see it, so I think I will continue to drain the life-blood of the wonderful people of that big generous city, with the golden pavements. Everything has gone according to schedule, but my friend Serurubele is just about the most miserable man on earth. The trouble with him is that he is one of those people who lack imagination, he always sees the dull side of life.

Serurubele is a fool as well as a hypocrite; if he is forced to beg, I wonder who forces him to hand over everything he receives. His honesty is so appalling it could make a bishop turn green with envy.

'One of these days I'm going to kill myself,' Serurubele says. 'I can't go on like this, I'm tired of being a parasite. Why did this have to happen to me, tell me, Nathan, why?'

How this man expects me to answer a question like this is beyond me. For one unguarded moment I almost told him to send his maker a telegram, and ask him all about it, but my gentler nature sees the harm such an answer can do.

'I don't know, Richard,' I say. 'But things like this happen; it is not in us to question why. Nature has a way of doing things and even then she gives something in return.'

This is one of the times I cannot find something concrete to say. I want to show him that there is compensation for his disability, but I cannot just lay my hands on it. This, I remembered, is what made me leave home.

I left home because my parents did not understand, they almost made me a neurotic. They were afraid to walk freely about the house, everybody sat down as if the house was full of cripples. They treated me like a new-born babe, all the things I wanted were brought to me, I was not even allowed to get myself some water. This excessive kindness gradually began to irritate me, it became a constant reminder that I did not belong, that I was an invalid. It then became apparent that they would soon put the food into my mouth, run my jaws up and down, and push it down my throat. This idea gave me my cue, I packed my things and left.

A new life opened for me. I got myself a wife, a property in Pampoenfontein, and a room in Sophiatown complete with piano. Within two years I had begged well over a hundred pounds. The money has been used wisely. Only one problem confronts me now, I want enough of it to provide for my old age.

I say good night and go to my room. After having something to eat I settle down to do some thinking.

The following morning I am at Room 14 bright and early. A white man with a bored expression is sitting behind a big mahogany desk. I tell him my name. He takes a paper and writes something on it. He tells me to go to that address. The faint showers that were falling outside have become heavier, and as I go out I say something nasty about the weather. A brilliant idea strikes me as a well-dressed lady is walking towards me. She looks like one of those people with a heart of gold. I put on a gloomy face, bend lower than usual and let my deformed carcass shiver.

She stops and looks at me as if she is responsible for my deformity.

'Why, you poor boy, you're almost freezing to death. Here, go buy yourself something to eat.' I feel the half crown in my hand, give her the usual line of how the Lord will bless, and send her a cartload of luck. From the way she is dressed she appears to have had more than her share of luck.

I play this trick all the way to the address I am given, and by the time I get there I can count well over ten half-crowns. Not bad, I say to myself, at this rate I can become the richest and most famous beggar in the city; to think that the department wants to pin me behind a desk, the idea is criminal.

I find the place and go in. My heart almost misses a beat when I see the large number of people inside. Some, if not most of them, are deformed monstrosities like myself. What could be more sweeter, I say to myself, not even unheard melodies. I can almost see my plan taking shape.

The man in charge starts explaining a few things about the machine. I pretend to be very interested and ask many unnecessary questions, but intelligent enough to impress him. By five o'clock I am running over the keyboard like a brilliant amateur.

On my way home I go via Serurubele's corner, he is still there and looking as miserable as usual. I suggest that we go home. I lure him to my room and when we get there I begin playing the piano like Rubinstein. Either my rendering is good or my friend just loves bad sounds.

'You can have a house like this and everything that goes with it. It's yours for the taking. Why beg for other people when you can do it for yourself?'

'Don't say such things about my people, I've got to help with the rent and the food,' Serurubele says. 'How do you think I am going to get a room like this? I can't just wish for it.'

'You don't have to, you must plan and work for it like I did.'

Last night I dreamt I was at the race-course and I saw the winning double as plain as I see my twisted leg. I raid my savings in the room and make my way to Turffontein. When I get there I start scouting around for policemen. None are around, and a soothing satisfaction comes with the realisation that I will not have to hide every time I see a police badge. I put a pound win on two and seven, a double in the first leg.

I am too nervous to watch the race, so I decide to walk about and appreciate Nature. Suddenly I feel like someone is watching me. I turn round and look right at Miss Gallovidian, a welfare worker, who has an uncanny habit of showing up at the most unexpected moments. I do not need a fortune-teller to tell me that I am in trouble. She has a notorious record of having safely deposited more than twenty beggars in the Refuge. My only chance is to get out of here before she can find a policeman.

I am going to the gate when I hear somebody talking about two and seven. For a moment I even forget the trouble Miss Gallovidian is going to bring me. I run as fast as a man with a twisted leg can to the bookie. Only six tickets were sold, everyone was trying to say, only I was not interested. In about half an hour I am at the building society where I deposit a sum of £670. After doing that, I take the taxi back to the course. This is my lucky day; another bit of luck like this, then I can retire to my property, and live happily thereafter with my wife. I can destroy my past and start a new life.

But too late!

I feel a gentle but firm hold on my arm. I jerk myself violently and try to hide among the people. I run for a few seconds, stumble and fall on my face. The policeman bends down, puts bracelets on my wrists, and whispers softly. 'Look, John, let's not have trouble! Come along quietly, and everything will be just fine!'

Under the circumstances I have no choice but to submit. My mother always told me never to resist arrest, let alone striking a uniformed officer of the law. My submission caused me to spend a not-so-glorious weekend in gaol.

I am almost certain that you will be back here in a few days, the magistrate had said. Somebody ought to tell him that he has a greater future . . . reading people's palms. He looks at me and a grin spreads over his pancake-like face. This place must be short of magistrates. Why has it got to be the same one all the time?

'It grieves me, but you leave me no alternative,' the magistrate says. 'Beggars who play the horses are a dangerous nuisance, they misuse the kindness that is showed to them. You have made begging a profession, and it is my duty to curb this occupation of yours. I am forced to send you to the Bantu Refuge.'

The van takes a turn into the grounds of the Refuge. There is nothing to comment about this place; it is completely encircled by trees, which give it an atmosphere of isolation and nonchalance. The van stops in front of the main entrance. The building looks like one of those dull fourteenth-century fortresses, with cobwebs in every closet.

Today I am celebrating my first four weeks at this sanatorium, four weeks of loneliness. No one has been to see me. My first two weeks I spent in entertaining my ego with a daring escape; but now my spirits are dulled by the hopelessness of such an attempt. The nearest town is ten miles away.

I am still ruminating when old man Rantolo comes paddling along on his seat. He is about the oldest man in the Refuge; his face is always sparkling with joy, and he has a way of making people believe that there is good in the world.

'There is someone to see you, Nathaniel, he says he's a friend of yours.'

I thank the old man and go to the reception-room. Richard Serurubele is the last person I expected to see, seeing him is a real comfort. I shake his hand as if he is a long-lost relation; his dull face lights up, and the firmness of his hand reassures me that the feeling is mutual.

'It's nice to see you, Nathan, the town is not the same without you.' His voice does not sound as warm as his face. 'I have a letter for you; I thought it might be important, so I brought it along myself . . . besides, I wanted to see you.'

'Thanks, Richard, I like the way you said that.' I tear the envelope and start reading. Tears flood my eyes as I read the second paragraph.

> Our son Tommy is dead . . . the doctor said he died from influenza. When it all started I thought he was running a temperature. Gradually the fever made him so weak that he could hardly eat; when the doctor came, it was too late.
>
>   Please come home Nathan, I'm frightened. Terry is also acting strangely . . . I can't stand it any more, please come home.

I had always said that only a miracle could get me out of here, but this time I have to go, miracle or no miracle, I just have to go.

'Is anything wrong, Nathan, why do you look so blank?'

'I have lost a son.'

'I'm sorry, Nathan, I wish I could have saved you all this. Things are bad enough without you having to lose your son.'

'What do you mean?'

'Your landlady has locked your room and is threatening to sell your things,' Serurubele says. 'She claims that you have not paid your rent for two months.'

I grab him by the neck and shake him violently. 'My piano . . . will she sell that too?'

He nods his head. I loosen my hold and stare at him viciously. That piano means everything to me, nobody is going to cheat me of it. It is the one concrete proof that I can work for what I want, just like any other man; it represents my entire life.

Serurubele conveys his regrets and goes away. A pathetic image of my wife flashes before me. She must have gone through a terrible ordeal. The being alone must have done her more harm than anything else.

Mr Lherzolite, the superintendent, looks at me with sympathetic eyes, as he reads my letter.

'I simply have to go home, Mr Lherzolite, my wife needs me,' I say. 'Please, sir, I'm trying to make you understand that my son is dead; that my wife is all by herself.'

'Look, Nathaniel, it's not my will that rules here,' he says. 'I only work here, I do not make the decisions. The least I can do is to write to the Welfare Society, telling them of your request.'

This arrangement will take about a week to complete; there is nothing else to do but wait. I thank him and go up to my room, and begin writing a long letter to my wife and to my father.

I choke with joy when I am told to report to Mr Lherzolite in his office. There are five important people in the office, at least they look important to me.

'These gentlemen are going to ask you some questions,' Mr Lherzolite says. 'You will listen to what they have to say, and answer them truthfully. Do you understand?'

I nod and look at their cold faces. The inquisition lasted for about an hour.

'Go and wait outside, Nathaniel,' Mr Lherzolite says.

They took ten minutes to arrive at a decision. Mr Lherzolite calls me in.

'It is the decision of this board that you be sent home. You are not to enter the area of Johannesburg without the approval of the Non-European Department,' Mr Lherzolite says. 'You are forbidden to beg within its jurisdiction. Your parents should be here any day, they are to be responsible for you.'

My wife is waving to us as we enter the gate of the farm. She has not changed a bit. She still has that radiant face, which often caused me to wonder why so beautiful a girl should ever marry a broken-down tramp like me. The day she said yes, I concluded that she was an amnesia case.

She runs to me and throws her arms round my neck. We lock each other in an embrace which isolates us from the rest of the world; her violently palpitating bosom is beating the tempo of a song of surrender. I kiss her long on the neck then our lips meet in the warmth of a kiss. The fire of her lips tells a tale of long, empty nights.

This tender scene is finally broken by a soft pat on my shoulder. My father smiles and beckons for us to come into the house. I ask about my child, everybody starts assuring me that everything is under control, and that a proper doctor has been in to see him.

'Nathaniel, my boy,' my father says, 'I have a surprise for you. If you will please step into the living-room.'

Standing in one corner of the room is my good old piano. My suitcase drops down, my mouth gaping like a sea-perch. My heart is beating so fast I feel like dancing the Zulu war and going savage. I rush to it throwing my arms round it in a tender embrace. Everyone is applauding as if expecting a recital from Beethoven's 'Moonlight Sonata'. I remove the top of the piano, rip off the back, and open a little panel hidden between the chords and the left covering.

'This is a day of surprises,' I say, casting a quick glance at them, and opening the little packet I took out of the panel. 'It is only fitting that one surprise should follow another.'

I empty the contents of the packet on the small table in the centre of the room. My entire savings heap on the table ... £183. My father's eyes pop as if in the act of falling out of the sockets.

'This is only cigarette-money, wait and see what I have saved up as the surprise to top all surprises.' I open my suitcase and take out the money I won at the race-course. 'Do you remember, father, I asked you to stop at the building society the day you came to take me from that place? Well, this is the reason I asked to stop there.' This time, even my mother becomes a statue of amazement.

I do not have to ask my father how the piano got here. The conspiracy is all over his face. I find it difficult to hold back my tears when I read the message in his eyes. Welcome home, my son, his eyes said.

We cannot give the accounts of all our informants, including one who had stabbed three people before he was caught shoplifting at the age of 13; but here is a typical story, of Jeremiah Majola, who tells us just how his shameful career came to an end at the age of 15:

'I was born in Randfontein and my parents moved to Alexandra when I was still very young. I went to school when I was 10 but already I had heard about picking pockets and snatching handbags.

'Our heroes were the boys who could steal and stab. The more stabbings they did, the bigger they were. The "biggest shot" of all was the one who had killed somebody – either with a knife or a gun.

'These boys used to have a lot of money and they were able to have a good time with the girls and buy them many presents. It was not long before I wanted to be a tsotsi.

'I was about 13 when I committed my first crime. My friend and I were drinking pineapple brew in Alexandra. It is made with mtombo, pineapple, sugar, oats, carbide and so on.

'The quick-service brew is made at 6.30 in the evening and can be swallowed just after. A glass jar for carrying fruit full of pineapple brew costs a shilling. I used to get drunk after about a gallon.

'The first time I got drunk my friend and I decided to go and steal something. We went over to the Inanda Club. It was a Sunday afternoon and all the white people were watching the game they play with horses. We each had a six-inch knife.

'I saw some Africans working near the club house and said: "Hey folks, I'm looking for a job."

'They told me to come back the next morning and see the boss.

'As I talked to them I looked in the door of the secretary's office and saw a lady's handbag and a grey sports jacket lying on a chair. I went in and took them.

'I was walking away when one of the stable boys shouted at me to put the things back in the office. I told him to come and get them himself and threw the bag and the coat on the ground. As he bent down to pick them up I stabbed him with my knife three times in the back – one up near his neck, the other in his ribs and the other in his buttocks. My friend and I picked up the things and ran away.

'We crossed the road near the club and saw a servant girl in the back yard of the house belonging to Mrs—. My friend asked the girl for a drink of water and when she went to the tap to get it I walked into the kitchen door.

'I was looking for money, but could find none. But in one of the bedrooms, under a pillow, I found a Baby Browning gun. This was better than money.

'I took it out to my friend. "Listen," I said. "I've got something very important. I'm going to make money out of this." And I showed him the gun. There were five bullets in it.

'We went to work at Bramley. Always we had something to drink or smoked some dagga to give us a big heart.

'Every Friday and Saturday we held up somebody at Bramley. Mostly they were Europeans, and nearly always in daylight.

'Why did I do it? Because I wanted to be a big shot among my friends and my girl-friends. I wanted a lot of money to have a good time and give my girls a good time. Sometimes I made £50 in one day with the gun. I would spend it all in three or four days and then go and get some more.

'When I leave Diepkloof I am going straight. I hope to get a good job. I have stabbed 15 or 16 people – sometimes when I robbed them and sometimes when one of my friends didn't have any money to buy me drink. But all that is finished now.

'I think the best way not to start stealing and stabbing is not to make friends with a boy who has got a bad spirit. He says to you, "What a fool you are. You only can make a few pounds a month while I can get £50 a day and all the girls I want."

'It's not our parents' fault. They don't even know we are doing it. Sometimes they think we are working or still at school. We always sleep at our homes.'

Well, there is his tale; a tale of wasted and degraded life. Decent citizens struggle to keep our African society straight, the police struggle, and reformatories like Diepkloof make great and noble efforts to turn young prisoners into good and upright citizens. Diepkloof takes in 600 youths: but there are perhaps 20,000 tsotsis, probably more, along the Reef. All these efforts are good, right and useful: but the roots of crime are to be found in the deep social evils that breed wickedness wherever they are found in the world.

Mob Passion

D CAN THEMBA 1953

Can Themba began his writing life by winning a short-story competition organised by *The Drum* and later became the magazine's assistant editor. He was born in Marabastad in 1924 and was a graduate of the African university, Fort Hare. It had been said of him that 'more than any other single member of the "Drum" staff he typified the "new urban culture"'. This story is a kind of South African 'Romeo and Juliet' tale. Tribal divisions run deep and the two lovers in the story find that the divisions between their tribes and families lead to inevitable tragedy and violence. Like the previous tale it marks how, in the 1950s, South Africa slipped into a period of ever-escalating violence and mob passion as a consequence of the years of repression. This led to violence not only between Black and White but amongst and between various groups of Blacks themselves.

There was a thick crowd on Platform Two, rushing for the 'All Stations' Randfontein train. Men, women and children were pushing madly to board the train. They were heaving and pressing, elbows in faces, bundles bursting, weak ones kneaded. Even at the opposite side people were balancing precariously to escape being shoved off the platform. Here and there deft fingers were exploring unwary pockets. Somewhere an outraged dignity was shrieking stridently, vilely cursing someone's parentage. The carriages became fuller and fuller. With a jerk the electric train moved out of the station.

'Whew!' sighed Linga Sakwe. He gathered his few parcels upon his lap, pressing his elbows to his side pockets. He did not really have any valuables in these pockets; only long habit was working instinctively now.

Linga was a tall, slender fellow, more man than boy. He was not particularly handsome; but he had those tense eyes of the young student who was ever inwardly protesting against some wrong or other. In fact at the moment he was not a student at all. He was working for a firm of lawyers in Market Street. He hoped to save enough money in a year or two to return to

Bus Stop, 1982

university to complete an arts degree which he had been forced by 'circumstances' to abandon.

People were still heaving about in the train but Linga was not annoyed. He knew that by the time the train reached Langlaagte, or Westbury, most of these folks would be gone and he would be able to breathe again. At Braamfontein many people alighted; but he was not thinking of his discomfort any more. He was thinking of Mapula now. She had promised that she would be in time for this train. That depended, of course, on whether she had succeeded in persuading the staff nurse in charge of the ward in which she worked to let her off early.

The train slowed down. Industria. Linga anxiously looked outside. Sure enough, there she was! He gave a wolf-whistle, as if he were admiring some girl he did not know. She hurried to his carriage, stepped in and sat beside him. They seemed not to know each other from Adam. An old man nearby was giving a lively account, in the grimmest terms, of the murders committed in Newclare.

At Westbury the atmosphere was tense. Everybody crowded at the windows to see. Everywhere there were white policemen, heavily armed. The situation was 'under control', but everyone knew that in the soul of almost every being in this area raved a seething madness, wild and passionate, with the causes lying deep. No cursory measures could remedy; no superficial explanation could illuminate. These jovial faces that could change into masks of bloodlust and destruction without warning, with the smallest provocation! There is a vicious technique faithfully applied in these riots. Each morning these people quietly rise, and with a businesslike manner hurry to their work. Each evening they return to a Devil's Party, uncontrollably drawn into hideous orgies. Sometimes the violence would subside for weeks or months, and then suddenly would flare up at some unexpected spot, on some unexpected pretext.

At Newclare, too, from the train all seemed quiet. But Linga and Mapula knew the deceptive quiet meant the same even here. The train rushed on, emptier. Only when they had passed Maraisburg did these two venture to speak to each other. Linga was Xhosa and Mapula Sotho. A Letebele and a Russian! They had to be very careful! Love in its mysterious, often ill-starred ways had flung them together.

Linga spoke first.

'Sure you saw no one who might know you?' he asked softly.

'Eh-eh,' she replied.

She fidgeted uneasily with the strap of her handbag. His hand went out and closed over her fingers. They turned simultaneously to look at each other.

A sympathetic understanding came into Linga's eyes. He smiled.

'Rather tense, isn't it?' he said.

She looked past him through the window.

'Witpoortjie!' she exclaimed. 'Come, let's go.'

She rose and went to the door. The train stopped and they went out. Together they walked to a bridge, went over the line and out by a little gate. For some two hundred yards they walked over flat, stubbly ground. Then they went down a mountain-cleft at the bottom of which ran a streamlet. They found a shady spot and sat down on the green grass. Then suddenly they fled into each other's arms like frightened children. The time-old ritual, ancient almost as the hills, always novel as the ever-changing skies. For a long time they clung to each other silently. Only the little stream gurgled its nonsense; these two daring hearts were lost to each other. The world, too – good, bad or indifferent – was forgotten in the glorious flux of their souls meeting and mingling.

At last Mapula spoke – half cried: 'Oh, Linga! I'm afraid.'

'*Here where the world is quiet?*' he quoted, with infinite softness. 'No, dear, nothing can reach and harm us here.' Then with a sigh: 'Still, the cruellest thing they do is to drive two young people like guilty things to sneak off only to see each other. What is wrong with our people, Mapula?'

She did not answer. He lay musing for a long time. She could see that he was slowly getting angry. Sometimes she wished she could understand the strange indignations of his spirit and the great arguments by which he explained life. Most times she only yearned for his love.

'They do not see! They do not see!' he continued vehemently. 'They butcher one another, and they seem to like it. Where there should be brotherhood and love, there are bitter animosities. Where there should be co-operation in common adversity, there are barriers of hostility, steeling a brother's heart against a brother's misery. Sometimes, 'Pule, I understand it. We have had so many dishonest leaders, and we have so often had our true leaders left in the lurch by weak-kneed colleagues and lukewarm followers, that no one wishes to stick his neck out too far. Where is the courage to weld these suicidal factions into a nation? The trouble is, very few of us have a vision comprehensive enough of our destiny! I believe *God has a few of us to whom He whispers in the ear*! Our true history is before us, for we yet have to build, to create, to achieve. Our very oppression is the flower of opportunity. If not for History's Grand Finale, why then does God hold us back? Hell! and here we are, feuding in God's dressing-room even before the curtain rises. Oh! – ' He covered his face and fell into her lap, unable to say any more.

Instinctively Mapula fingered his hair. In God's dressing-room, she thought. What does it mean? But his anguish stabbed at her heart. Trying to forget herself she only sought within her a tenderness to quell the bitter wretchedness she had heard in his voice.

'Linga, no! Let me show you something else – something that I understand. It is not so long before you and I can marry, I dream about the home that we are going to have. I . . . I want that home, Linga. You taught me that woman's greatest contribution to civilisation so far has been to furnish homes where great men and great ideas have developed. Moreover, there's our problem. Let us rather think of ways of handling my father. No, no; not now. Let us think about the present, about *now*.'

Thabo was running faster now that he was nearing home. His mind was in a whirl; but he knew that he had to tell his father. The lopsided gate was in the far corner, so he smartly leaped over the fence where it was slack. He stopped abruptly at the door. He always did when there were people. But now he soon realised these people were his two uncles – Uncle Alpheus and Uncle Frans. Somehow great news always brings a glory of prestige on the head of the bringer. Thabo felt himself almost a hero now; for these two men were diehard stalwarts in the Russian cause. Uncle Alpheus was a romantic firebrand while Uncle Frans was a scheming character of the power-behind-the-throne variety. They were complementary to each other: together a formidable team.

'Father, where is he?' hissed Thabo, breathing hard. The excitement in his voice aroused everyone.

'Holy Shepherd! What's the matter, boy?' cried Uncle Alpheus.

'Mapula, Mapula. She loves with a Letebele.'

'What!' exploded Uncle Alpheus. 'Where is she?' Then more calmly: 'Come'n, boy. Tell us everything more quietly; your father is out there?'

'J-J-Jonas t-t-tells me – J-Jonas is a boy who works with me – Jonas tells me that Mapula loves with a Letebele. They always meet at the hospital; but never in the sitting-room. He hopes to marry her.'

'Never!' barked Alpheus. Just then the door burst open. A party of men carried in the limp form of Thabo's father. He was unconscious and blood streamed all over his face. Beyond them, just outside the door, a crowd had gathered. Everyone was at once asking what had happened. As the news spread, ugly moods swept the crowd. Ra-Thabo was carried into the bedroom and tended by the women. Alpheus and Frans returned to the fore-room and conferred.

'What now?' Alpheus asked Frans.

'Of course, we must revenge. You will talk to the people – the women. Talk fire into them. Connect it with the Mapula business; that'll warm them. Suggest drugs – a Letebele must use drugs, mustn't he? I'll be in the house. Just when they begin to get excited I'll arrange to carry Ra-Thabo out – to the hospital, you know. See if we can't get them bad!' He smiled cheerlessly.

Outside, the crowd – mostly women – was thickening. Even in the streets they could be seen coming along in groups, blanketed men and women. From the house Thabo and his little sister, Martha, joined the crowd. It was obvious that their uncles were going to do something about it.

Alpheus stepped onto the little mud wall. He raised his left hand and the blanket over it rose with it. This movement was most dramatic. In a few moments the crowd moved closer to him and became silent. Then he began to speak. He began in a matter-of-fact voice, giving the bare fact that Ra-Thabo, their leader, had been hurt. Warming gradually he discussed the virtues of this man. Then he went on to tell of how this man had actually been hurt. Neither confused fighting nor cowardly brutalities rose in the mind as this man spoke, but a glorious picture of crusaders charging on in a holy cause behind their lion-hearted leader. Oh, what a clash there was! The Letebele were pushed beyond Westbury station. There the heroes met a rested, reinforced enemy. For a moment all that could be seen was the head of Ra-Thabo going down among them. The clang of battle could be heard; the furious charge could be seen, in the words of this man who was not there. The Basothos fought desperately and won so much ground that their all-but-lost leader could be rescued and carried back home. And what finds he there? Alpheus's voice went down softer and heavier, touching strings of pathos, rousing tragic emotions which the hearts present had never before experienced. There was an automatic movement in the crowd as everybody strained forward to hear. In awful, horror-filled whispers he told of Ra-Thabo's daughter giving herself to a Letebele. The thing is not possible! he hissed. It would not have happened if the maid had not been bewitched with drugs. Are they going to brook it! he cracked. No! all the throats roared. Are they ready for vengeance! Now! thundered the mob. Someone in the crowd shouted 'Mule!' Then the women took up their famous war-cry, chilling to a stranger, but driving the last doubting spirit there to frenzy and fury.

'Ee! – le! – le! – le! – le! – le! – le! – Eu! – Eu! – Eu!'

Now they were prancing and swaying in uninterpretable rhythms. A possessed bard in their midst was chattering the praises of the dead, the living and the unborn; his words clattering like the drumsticks of a fiend.

'Let us go past Maraisburg and attack them from the rear!' yelled Alpheus over the din.

At that moment the door of the house went open. The mob, which had been on the point of dashing out, recoiled. The sight they saw stunned them. Frans and two other men were carrying out Ra-Thabo, besmeared with blood. Thabo saw Uncle Alpheus leaping with trailing blanket and yelling 'To Maraisburg!' Again he leaped over the fence into the street. The mob followed hard on his heels.

'MULE!' 'MULE!' 'MULE!'

As the last blanket swept round the corner, Frans turned back to the injured man. His two helpers had also been drawn in by the irresistible suction of the mob-feeling. With a smile he said to the unhearing Ra-Thabo: 'I'll have to get a taxi to take you to hospital, brother.' Then he carried him back into the house.

'All Change! All Change!' And more brusquely: 'Come'n. Puma! Puma!'

Linga and Mapula hurried out. News had arrived that trouble had started again at Newclare; more seriously than usual. All trains from Randfontein were being stopped here and sent back.

Shrugging, Linga drew Mapula away, and arm-in-arm they strolled along the platform, out by the little gate, into some suburban area. For a time they walked on in silence. Then Mapula spoke. 'I hope I'll get back in time,' she said.

'Then let's walk faster. We might get a lift outside the suburb.' They walked into the open country. Linga knew that if he could only find a certain golf-course somewhere around here, he would know where the road was. Meanwhile, they had to stumble on over rough country, and Mapula's cork-heeled shoes were tormenting her toes. She limped on as stoically as she could. Linga did not notice her suffering as he was looking out for familiar landmarks. Those trees looked suspiciously like the golf-course to him.

When they reached the trees Mapula said: 'Linga, let us rest here; my toes are suffering.'

'All right,' he replied. 'But I must look for the road. Let's look for a cool place where you may rest while I search for the golf-course.'

'Mm.'

He led her amongst the trees. She sat down and pulled off her shoes. When he thought he saw a shadow of distress flit across her brow he bent down, took her hand, pressed it and muttered: 'Back in a moment, sweet.' He rose slowly, looked at her indecisively, then turned away slowly and walked off.

He did not search far before he noticed a torn and faded flag. The hole was nearby. Suddenly he emerged from the cluster of trees, and came upon the road. But his attention was caught by a horde of Russians pursuing a woman who came flying towards Linga. This spelt trouble for the Letebele. But in a flash he thought of an idea. He spoke fluent Sesotho and believed he could pass for a Mosotho, possibly as a Russian. He quickly drew a white handkerchief from the pocket of his trousers, tied it round his head. This made him look like an active supporter of the Russian cause. Skirts flying, the woman sped past him. Facing the mob he shouted: 'Helele!'

All its wrath spent, the mob crowded round out of sheer curiosity. Some were even in a jocular mood now; one playing lustily on a concertina. But here and there Linga could see deadly weapons snatched up in their hasty exodus from Newclare. He spoke to them in fluent Sesotho, taking his idiom from Teyateyaneng. He asked if he was on the road to Newclare; he said that he worked in Roodepoort, but was going to Newclare because his uncle there wanted more man-power in the house. Won't they please tell him where this road was?

'Che! It is no Letebele this; this is a child of our home,' remarked Alpheus.

'Kgele! You speak it, man,' said a burly fellow. Then everyone directed Linga to Newclare.

Just then Mapula came running, shoes in hand and stockings twisted round her neck.

'Linga! Linga, my darling! What are they doing to you!' she screamed as she forced her way through the crowd. Linga stiffened. When she reached him she flung her arm around him and clung to him with all her strength, crying all the time. Then she saw her uncle, stupefied like the rest of them, standing there. She ran to him and begged him to save her lover. He pushed her aside, walked up to Linga, and stood before him, arms akimbo.

'Ehe! So you *are* a Letebele after all. You lie so sleekly that I can understand why my daughter thinks she loves you.' Then he swung round, his blanket trailing in an arc. 'Friends, we need go no further. This is the dog that bewitched my brother's child. Let's waste no time with him. Tear him to pieces!' The mob rushed upon Linga: '*Mmate! Mmate!*'

'Uncle! Uncle!' cried Mapula. But even as she cried she knew that nothing could be done. She had courted the contempt of her people; and she understood now that all her entreaties were falling upon deaf ears. Whether from convenience or superstition – it did not signify which – she was considered the victim of the Letebele's root-craft.

Suddenly from the scuffling mob flew an axe which fell at her feet. In a flash she knew her fate. Love, frustrated beyond bearing, bent her mind to the horrible deed.

Mapula acted. Quickly she picked up the axe whilst the mob was withdrawing from its prey, several of them spattered with blood. With the axe in her hand Mapula pressed through them until she reached the inner, sparser group. She saw Alpheus spitting upon Linga's battered body. He turned with a guttural cackle – He-he-he! He-he-he! – into the descending axe. It sank into his neck and down he went. She stepped on his chest and pulled out the axe. The blood gushed out all over her face and clothes. With that evil-looking countenance she gradually turned to the stunned crowd, half lifting the axe and walking slowly but menacingly towards the largest group. They retreated – a hundred and twenty men and women retreated before this devil-possessed woman with the ghastly appearance. But then she saw the mangled body of the man she loved and her nerve snapped. The axe slipped from her hand and she dropped on Linga's body, crying piteously: 'Jo-o! Jo-o! Jo-o! Jo-na-jo! Jo-na-jo!'

Someone came and lifted her up. Someone else was dragging Alpheus's bleeding corpse by the collar so that his shoes sprang out one after the other.

The crowd was going back now. All the bravado gone, they were quiet and sulky. Only the agonised wailing of Mapula could be heard. Every breast was quelled by a sense of something deeply wrong, a sense of outrage. The tumult in every heart, feeling individually now, was a human protest insistently seeking expression, and then that persistent wail of the anguished girl, torturing the innermost core of even the rudest conscience there. The men felt themselves before God; the women heard the denunciations of thwarted love. Within they were all crying bitterly: 'Jo-o! Jo-o! Jo-nana-jo!'

Fanyan

EZEKIEL MPHAHLELE 1957

This is one of a sequence of stories which the Black writer, Mphahlele, born in 1919 and brought up in an urban ghetto in Pretoria, published under the general title of 'Lesane'. Fanyan is a member of the Lesane household, young and inexperienced for his age, and this story shows him beginning to grow up bewildered by the difficult world around him. The story celebrates innocence in the midst of a world of corruption. 'Dagga', mentioned here and in several other stories, is an illegal drug, like cannabis, widely used and sold on the streets.

Fanyan felt awkward and clumsy being in Form 1 at the age of 18. 'Hey, you goat!' the arithmetic master said. 'You, there, don't be such a clumsy owl!' shouted the English mistress. 'No, no, no, we don't construct a triangle like that. Where were you born?' the mathematics master said. Fanyan felt a wild storm rage inside him especially when the girls of his class said: 'Shame!' and clicked their tongues with pity. They made him feel as if he were soft.

He knew he couldn't do high school work fast enough. His schooling had been retarded in the country, where there was so much hoeing and harvesting to do in between school terms. They hadn't told him at home why they had suddenly changed their decision to let him work. In order that his conscience should sit easy Lesane ordered Fanyan to stay at school for about a year. 'It will add to his country education. I went to country school myself. Did me no good.'

'Wai, Elisha, you used to write to me when you were courting,' said his wife.

'Yes, yes, but nothing more.'

Fanyan's going to school was part of the little reorganisation in the Lesane home. Ma-Lesane started to do white people's washing. The eldest of the three brats, a 9-year-old boy, was sent to the Anglican nursery school two streets down. Fanyan had to carry the washing to the suburbs after school, the mother fetched it on Mondays.

He had just delivered washing at a suburban house one afternoon when somebody called him from the other side of the road. It was a policeman.

Fanyan stopped. He sensed that the policeman wanted him to cross over to him.

'Where's your pass?' the constable said sharply.

The lad searched all his pockets. Then it suddenly flashed into his head that he had left it at home. He gaped at the constable. He tried to plead. Just then the pick-up van swerved maliciously round the corner and came up to them like a dog that had been sniffing for something and suddenly located it.

'Bung him in!' said the driver, a white policeman.

'Please, please, my pass is at home. Please, please, we can go and fetch it.'

The constables laughed heartily. 'Bung him in! Throw him in!' one shouted. Fanyan was thrown in.

Inside there was a crowd of others. It took time for his eyes to adjust themselves to the dark. When he could see the faces he couldn't recognise anyone. He was in a fright. He wanted to jump out, but there was a strong gauze-wire barrier at the entrance.

The night in the cells was enough to give Fanyan a foretaste of the wrath of the law in all its frowning terror. A man from another batch was taken to the charge office at the end of the passage. He came out puffed, with purple eyes. Ripping laughter. Prayerful stuttering lips. Agonising thuds. Gasping, knee-buckling fright. Cheeky passive snorting. He saw and heard them all within those greasy walls that looked like the devil's own spitting ground.

The policeman who stood next to Fanyan's batch and kept prodding one here and another there in the ribs smiled when he saw how terrified the youngster was. Poor fellow, how green he is still, the policeman was thinking.

Out in the country Fanyan had actually stood five yards away from a mounted policeman. He remembered how frightened he had been of the law that stood erect on four large hoofs and great lumps of animal muscle and stirrups and shining spurs. But he also remembered that it was not nearly as terrifying as the law on four wheels; the law that darted from one place to another with lightning effect on screeching tyres; the law that stretched out a large paw and caught you by the scruff of the neck; the law that often gave a long weird whining but sharp sound with a siren.

The next day Lesane paid ten shillings to have his son released. The police would not even look at the pass the old man brought. The fine, they said, was for failing to take out a pass when asked to.

A week later Fanyan was at Seleke's. There was something mysteriously charming about Seleke, Fanyan thought, even in the light of a candle, and she

often showed a sisterly affection for him. He got used to calling on her. Seleke
and her cousin had moved over from Nadia Street. 'Good for business,' as
Seleke explained it. Like all other shebeen queens she was believed to have
powerful contacts with the police. Fanyan reflected that perhaps it was just
that kind of boldness Seleke had which he lacked that charmed him.

Her cousin, known simply as 'Seleke's cousin' – nobody cared to find out
his real name – drank as much as ever. 'He simply can't help himself, poor
chap,' said old Mbata with the usual shock-absorbing piety. 'Kiss your elbow
if he doesn't wet his blankets at night,' Ma-Sibiya said. Lesane pointed to the
skies and said, 'A cow will give birth to a pig if that cousin of Seleke's doesn't
end up in a mental hospital.'

Seleke's cousin had ceased trying to help himself. He became more and
more stubborn against criticism. He didn't work in town. He just did odd
jobs at home for his keep, like digging holes for his cousin's beer, running
errands and keeping their two rooms clean. He had long stopped trying to
keep clean himself. His trousers were always either too small or too big for
him. Often one of the constables who drank at Seleke's gave him articles from
old police uniforms. 'The uncle with the government trousers,' boys would
say.

'You think I'm drunk, eh?' he said to Fanyan who sat opposite him in the
front room. He turned to lower the volume of the radiogram music at the
corner. 'Right, I'm drunk – hic. But I can speak English better than any of
them – hic. The bloody cheap swanks! Why the – hic – hell can't they leave me
alone? I live my own – hic – life, not theirs.'

Fanyan later understood that 'they' were the people who were supposed to
be talking of Seleke's cousin as an incorrigible drunk – just a useless
'hole-digger'. There was a tribe of such men in Newclare backyards who were
prepared to drift from one house to another as long as the people were
prepared to keep them while they dug holes for beer and kept watch against
the police. When people labelled a man 'hole-digger' they had given him up.
And then they looked at one another smugly, with the obvious satisfaction
that they had found a solution to an intricate puzzle.

Seleke came in from the back room. She gave her cousin a leg of chicken
and one to Fanyan. 'You're going to be a great man one day,' her cousin said,
pointing at Fanyan with the leg of chicken. He had no top front teeth, and his
tongue kept flicking out between the two fang-like canines. He tore the meat
with one fang and, with a sinew hanging down mischievously as far as the

chin, Seleke's cousin went over to Fanyan and leaned against him.

'Oh, leave the boy alone. Never!' Seleke said. Even when she was not disputing anything she said, 'Never!' Fanyan noticed that she was a little drunk. 'Don't mind him, Fanyan.'

One of the things Seleke's cousin had stopped trying to do was to argue with her. He removed himself timidly, but not before he issued the final warning to Fanyan: 'You'll be a great man one day.'

'Scared of the police, aren't you?' she said to Fanyan. He nodded.

'Never! You'll get used to it, don't worry. Just hold your heart in two hands. A police badge used to make my toes sweat. It's like looking at King George's medal now.' Then she told a frightening experience she had with the police when she was a girl. She got up to demonstrate with her arms that were shaped like a constable's baton. She had a heavy bust, and when she leaned over the table to support herself while laughing, Fanyan observed the division of her breasts. They parted where they united. At once bashfully, delicately and boldly. As she laughed the breasts seemed about to spill over the bodice of her frock, and Fanyan suppressed an instinctive urge to hold out his hands to prevent them from falling.

'Never!' she said without provocation.

'What gives you such a strong heart with the police coming in and out of your rooms?' Fanyan wanted to know. He marvelled at this 35-year-old round bundle of vitality that had a streak of ruthlessness as well.

'When you want to live, then you've got to have a tough heart. Never!'

'How did you begin?'

'Like most of us in the townships. School, no money, school, no money, out, factory, out, no money, marriage, out, lie, cheat, bribe, live. Nothing more. Never!'

Fanyan made to go. 'Heavens! Do something good for me, Fanyan. Do. You know Shigumbu, four houses down? Of course you do. Run down there and tell him to give you a small packet. Bring it here. Do. Almost forgot. Never!'

Fanyan left. A few minutes later he was knocking at a room in a backyard four houses down. Backyards, he observed, had their own peculiar life, with a continuous buzzing noise. Shigumbu opened the door. He was the dried-up bachelor from Nyasaland. After three years of city life he had decided that Johannesburg was 'rittel bit better than Nyasaland, bludder', quite aware that he was comparing a city with a country.

'From Seleke, are you not?' Fanyan nodded. Shigumbu looked groggy. He put a paper-wrapped packet into a glass jar, and gave it to Fanyan. He went about the room like a cat. 'Give her this.' The set of false teeth he had gave him an evil, snarling appearance when they touched the empty gums of the lower jaw.

Fanyan got out into the street. He was going to swerve in towards the row of houses when he saw a policeman standing not far from Seleke's room. His heart seemed to fall on a concrete base in the pit of his stomach. He made a visible movement to change his course and walked back into the street.

'Hey! Come here!' the policeman said, going towards Fanyan. The lad bolted, and the policeman followed. He passed his home and made for the cross-street. He jumped on to the stoep of Lai Tong's shop. Another policeman turned the corner from the opposite direction. Fanyan stopped. Fear choked him and seemed to spin him round like a top.

The policeman who saw him first wrenched the jar from his hand and took out the packet. He unwrapped it, put his nose to it and nodded several times. Dagga, as he thought.

'Whose is this?' the constable asked, as if he was bored.

'My sister's – Seleke's,' Fanyan managed to whisper.

'U-huh. Where's your home?' The lad pointed down the street.

'Come. We go there first.' He felt the policeman's grip tighten round his wrist. 'Thank you, brother,' the constable addressed his colleague.

Immediately the two entered the front room, Lesane stood up. Then Diketso and then Ma-Lesane stood up, her hands dovetailed together and lifted up to the chin.

'That boy is not my son! He's not my son, do you hear me?' As if he had spent the last atom of his energy saying those words, Lesane collapsed, unconscious.

Ma-Mafate turned her washtub round to face Ma-Ntoi.

'Didn't I tell you?' said Ma-Mafate, adjusting the petticoat string which kept slipping down the shoulders.

'What?' enquired Ma-Ntoi.

'That woman Seleke. A hundred Sodoms and Gomorrahs put together in the woman's rooms.'

'I still don't understand, she wasn't arrested.'

'See what I mean?'

'What?'

'She's in love with the policeman who caught that Lesane boy.'

'Oh, no.'

'What was he doing in front of her rooms?'

'Now I see.'

'My cousin in Nadia Street tells me these things. He knows all about her and the police.' She had tried so often to keep the petticoat string in place and she simply left it to hang.

'But are we to say every woman loves a policeman if he does not arrest her?'

'What else?'

'She can buy him over to keep his mouth shut.'

'But I hear they were two policemen?'

'Buy both. She's got the money.' But Ma-Ntoi knew that this sort of defence would merely whet her friend's appetite for more talk and speculation.

'My cousin says it must have been her lover standing in front of her place.'

'No one has so far told us he saw the policeman. Only Lesane's family saw him.'

'They wouldn't talk about it in any case, surely. Somebody else must have seen the policeman.'

Ma-Ntoi shrugged her shoulders.

'Else how did we get the news that Fanyan was caught by a policeman and that dagga was found in the jar he had and that he said it was Seleke's?'

Ma-Ntoi looked around as if to locate the source of the rumour. She didn't know, but these things travelled mysteriously, she said.

'Here's Old Mbata. We'll ask him,' Ma-Mafate whispered. They waited.

'Greetings, mothers.'

'Come over, let's hear something.' Old Mbata stepped over to the women.

'Give us a bite on the tip of the ear. We hear there's a bit of trouble in Lesane's house.'

'No trouble, woman. But Lesane's not well. You know he has had bad kidneys for a long time.'

Being cautious, eh? they both thought.

'This thing that happened last night?'

'Oh, that? Nothing much. Lesane's lad is dead scared of the police. He had a bottle of herbs and the young fool dug his toes into the ground when he saw a policeman. Well, they caught up with him. But they found it was only herbs.

Seleke's. One of these days that boy's going to scream in front of a policeman like a goat about to give birth.'

He shuffled off, thinking to himself: the babbling female creatures!

'The sly old man!' Ma-Ntoi said. 'He thinks we were born yesterday.'

As the news travelled, the story of Fanyan and the police changed in plot as often as in the style of telling it. Some were sure it was nothing more than herbs. 'That boy's going to be the death of his father,' others said. Shigumbu, the dried-up old bachelor, made sure that, in Rosa Street at least, the story should revolve round herbs.

'I bought the herbs at Mai Mai myself, bludder. For a cough. Well, if people want to think it's dagga let them, my bludder. Look at the moon and say it's a woman's breast, you can fly up and kiss it if you want it, bludder. I can't help it if the moon is not a breast, can I now? I didn't make the moon what it is. Solly, bludder.' He felt secure. Nobody could retrieve that dagga from the drain.

To Seleke, Shigumbu said: 'How could you send a rabbit-hearted fellow like that, sister?'

'Don't get excited, man,' said Seleke.

'Just think if the fellow wasn't the type whose tongue you can cut off with £20 – whew! I can't think of eighteen months in gaol, no fine, sister.'

Lesane took the better of an hour to come round. The sight of a son of his in the hands of the police was too much for him. Seleke came over the same night and then in the morning and got him to cool down. But the picture of a policeman and his son! He knew he couldn't easily forget it.

'I'm sorry it came to this, old father,' Seleke had said. 'Don't be hard on the lad. If only he doesn't lose his head when he sees a constable.'

'Why should he get used to seeing a policeman – to be the devil's messenger?'

'No, old father, because he'll see many more.'

'Look here, woman –' Lesane couldn't finish the sentence. He knew how true it was and felt the pain of it. He dismissed Seleke.

'Next week you must go out and look for work.' That was an instruction to Fanyan. 'No more school for you.' Fanyan was not displeased. He was only a little annoyed that it had to be announced with such tight-jawed gravity as if it were important. But he soon realised how important it was – in more ways than one.

A Drink in the Passage

ALAN PATON   1961

Alan Paton, who was born in Pietermaritzburg in 1903, is probably the best known of White South African writers outside his own country, largely through his *Cry the Beloved Country*. He was also of considerable political importance as the President for many years of the South African Liberal Party of which he was the founder. He was Principal of the Diepkloof Reformatory from 1935 to 1948 and the volume from which this story is taken (*Debbie Go Home*) contains a number of stories based upon his time there. This particular story well illustrates the helplessness felt by both people on either side of the colour bar during the worst period of apartheid.

In the year 1960 the Union of South Africa celebrated its Golden Jubilee, and there was a nation-wide sensation when the one-thousand-pound prize for the finest piece of sculpture was won by a black man, Edward Simelane. His work, 'African Mother and Child', not only excited the admiration, but touched the conscience or heart or whatever it is, of white South Africa, and was likely to make him famous in other countries.

It was by an oversight that his work was accepted, for it was the policy of the Government that all the celebrations and competitions should be strictly segregated. The committee of the sculpture section received a private reprimand for having been so careless as to omit the words 'for whites only' from the conditions, but was told, by a very high personage it is said, that if Simelane's work was indisputably the best, it should receive the award. The committee then decided that this prize must be given along with the others, at the public ceremony which would bring this particular part of the celebrations to a close.

For this decision it received a surprising amount of support from the white public, but in certain powerful quarters there was an outcry against any departure from the 'traditional policies' of the country, and a threat that many white prize-winners would renounce their prizes. However, a crisis was averted, because the sculptor was 'unfortunately unable to attend the ceremony'.

'I wasn't feeling up to it,' Simelane said mischievously to me. 'My parents, and my wife's parents, and our priest, decided that I wasn't feeling up to it. And finally I decided so too. Of course Majosi and Sola and the others wanted me to go and get my prize personally, but I said, "Boys, I'm a sculptor, not a demonstrator."'

'This cognac is wonderful,' he said, 'especially in these big glasses. It's the first time I've had such a glass. It's also the first time I've drunk a brandy so slowly. In Orlando you develop a throat of iron, and you just put back your head and pour it down, in case the police should arrive.'

He said to me, 'This is the second cognac I've had in my life. Would you like to hear the story of how I had my first?'

You know the Alabaster Bookshop in Von Brandis Street? Well, after the competition they asked me if they could exhibit my 'African Mother and Child'. They gave a whole window to it, with a white velvet backdrop, if there is anything called white velvet, and some complimentary words, '*Black man conquers white world*'.

Well somehow I could never go and look in that window. On my way from the station to the Herald office, I sometimes went past there, and I felt good when I saw all the people standing there, but I would only squint at it out of the corner of my eye.

Then one night I was working late at the Herald, and when I came out there was hardly anyone in the streets, so I thought I'd go and see the window, and indulge certain pleasurable human feelings. I must have got a little lost in the contemplation of my own genius, because suddenly there was a young white man standing next to me.

He said to me, 'What do think of that, mate?' And you know, one doesn't get called 'mate' every day.

'I'm looking at it,' I said.

'I live near here,' he said, 'and I come and look at it nearly every night. You know it's by one of your own boys, don't you? See, Edward Simelane.'

'Yes, I know.'

'It's beautiful,' he said. 'Look at that mother's head. She's loving that child, but she's somehow watching too. Do you see that? Like someone guarding. She knows it won't be an easy life.'

He cocked his head on one side, to see the thing better.

'He got a thousand pounds for it,' he said. 'That's a lot of money for one of your boys. But good luck to him. You don't get much luck, do you?'

Then he said confidentially, 'Mate, would you like a drink?'

Well honestly I didn't feel like a drink at that time of night, with a white stranger and all, and me still with a train to catch to Orlando.

'You know we black people must be out of the city by eleven,' I said.

'It won't take long. My flat's just round the corner. Do you speak Afrikaans?'

'Since I was a child,' I said in Afrikaans.

'We'll speak Afrikaans then. My English isn't too wonderful. I'm van Rensburg. And you?'

I couldn't have told him my name. I said I was Vakalisa, living in Orlando.

'Vakalisa, eh? I haven't heard that name before.'

By this time he had started off, and I was following, but not willingly. That's my trouble, as you'll soon see. I can't break off an encounter. We didn't exactly walk abreast, but he didn't exactly walk in front of me. He didn't look constrained. He wasn't looking round to see if anyone might be watching.

He said to me, 'Do you know what I wanted to do?'

'No,' I said.

'I wanted a bookshop, like that one there. I always wanted that, ever since I can remember. When I was small, I had a little shop of my own.' He laughed at himself. 'Some were real books, of course, but some of them I wrote myself. But I had bad luck. My parents died before I could finish school.'

Then he said to me, 'Are you educated?'

I said unwillingly, 'Yes'. Then I thought to myself, how stupid, for leaving the question open.

And sure enough he asked, 'Far?'

And again unwillingly, I said, 'Far.'

He took a big leap and said, 'Degree?'

'Yes.'

'Literature?'

'Yes.'

He expelled his breath, and gave a long 'Ah'. We had reached his building, Majorca Mansions, not one of those luxurious places. I was glad to see that the entrance lobby was deserted. I wasn't at my ease. I don't feel at my ease in such places, not unless I am protected by friends, and this man was a stranger. The lift was at ground level, marked 'Whites only. Slegs vir Blankes.' Van

Rensburg opened the door and waved me in. Was he constrained? To this day I don't know. While I was waiting for him to press the button, so that we could get moving and away from that ground floor, he stood with his finger suspended over it, and looked at me with a kind of honest, unselfish envy.

'You were lucky,' he said. 'Literature, that's what I wanted to do.'

He shook his head and pressed the button, and he didn't speak again until we stopped high up. But before we got out he said suddenly, 'If I had had a bookshop, I'd have given that boy a window too.'

We got out and walked along one of those polished concrete passageways, I suppose you could call it a stoep if it weren't so high up; let's call it a passage. On the one side was a wall, and plenty of fresh air, and far down below, Von Brandis Street. On the other side were the doors, impersonal doors; you could hear radios and people talking, but there wasn't a soul in sight. I wouldn't like living so high; we Africans like being close to the earth. Van Rensburg stopped at one of the doors, and said to me, 'I won't be a minute.' Then he went in, leaving the door open, and inside I could hear voices. I thought to myself, he's telling them who's here. Then after a minute or so, he came back to the door, holding two glasses of red wine. He was warm and smiling.

'Sorry there's no brandy,' he said. 'Only wine. Here's happiness.'

Now I certainly had not expected that I would have my drink in the passage. I wasn't only feeling what you may be thinking. I was thinking that one of the impersonal doors might open at any moment, and someone might see me in a 'white' building, and see me and van Rensburg breaking the liquor laws of the country. Anger could have saved me from the whole embarrassing situation, but you know I can't easily be angry. Even if I could have been, I might have found it hard to be angry with this particular man. But I wanted to get away from there, and I couldn't. My mother used to say to me, when I had said something anti-white, 'Son, don't talk like that, talk as you are.' She would have understood at once why I took a drink from a man who gave it to me in the passage.

Van Rensburg said to me, 'Don't you know this fellow Simelane?'

'I've heard of him,' I said.

'I'd like to meet him,' he said. 'I'd like to talk to him.' He added in explanation, 'You know, talk out my heart to him.'

A woman of about fifty years of age came from the room beyond, bringing a plate of biscuits. She smiled and bowed to me. I took one of the biscuits, but not for all the money in the world could I have said to her 'Dankie, my nooi', or that disgusting 'Dankie, missus', nor did I want to speak to her in English because her language was Afrikaans, so I took the risk of it and used the word '*mevrou*' for the politeness of which some Afrikaners would knock a black man down, and I said, in high Afrikaans, with a smile and a bow too, 'Ek is u dankbaar, mevrou.'

But nobody knocked me down. The woman smiled and bowed, and van Rensburg, in a strained voice that suddenly came out of nowhere, said, 'Our land is beautiful. But it breaks my heart.'

The woman put her hand on his arm, and said, 'Jannie, Jannie.'

Then another woman and a man, all about the same age, came up and stood behind van Rensburg.

'He's a B.A.,' van Rensburg told them. 'What do you think of that?'

The first woman smiled and bowed to me again, and van Rensburg said, as though it were a matter for grief, 'I wanted to give him brandy, but there's only wine.'

The second woman said, 'I remember, Jannie. Come with me.'

She went back into the room, and he followed her. The first woman said to me, 'Jannie's a good man. Strange, but good.'

And I thought the whole thing was mad, and getting beyond me, with me a black stranger being shown a testimonial for the son of the house, with these white strangers standing and looking at me in the passage, as though they wanted for God's sake to touch me somewhere and didn't know how, but I saw the earnestness of the woman who had smiled and bowed to me, and I said to her, 'I can see that, mevrou.'

'He goes down every night to look at the statue,' she said. 'He says only God could make something so beautiful, therefore God must be in the man who made it, and he wants to meet him and talk out his heart to him.'

She looked back at the room, and then she dropped her voice a little, and said to me, 'Can't you see, it's somehow because it's a black woman and a black child?'

And I said to her, 'I can see that, mevrou.'

She turned to the man and said of me, 'He's a good boy.'

Then the other woman returned with van Rensburg, and van Rensburg had a bottle of brandy. He was smiling and pleased, and he said to me, 'This isn't ordinary brandy, it's French.'

He showed me the bottle, and I, wanting to get the hell out of that place, looked at it and saw it was cognac. He turned to the man and said, 'Uncle, you remember? When you were ill? The doctor said you must have good brandy. And the man at the bottle-store said this was the best brandy in the world.'

'I must go,' I said. 'I must catch that train.'

'I'll take you to the station,' he said. 'Don't you worry about that.'

He poured me a drink and one for himself.

'Uncle,' he said, 'what about one for yourself?'

The older man said, 'I don't mind if I do', and he went inside to get himself a glass.

Van Rensburg said, 'Happiness', and lifted his glass to me. It was good brandy, the best I've ever tasted. But I wanted to get the hell out of there. I stood in the passage and drank van Rensburg's brandy. Then Uncle came back with his glass, and van Rensburg poured him a brandy, and Uncle raised his glass to me too. All of us were full of goodwill, but I was waiting for the opening of one of the impersonal doors. Perhaps they were too, I don't know. Perhaps when you want so badly to touch someone you don't care. I was drinking my brandy almost as fast as I would have drunk it in Orlando.

'I must go,' I said.

Van Rensburg said, 'I'll take you to the station.' He finished his brandy, and I finished mine too. We handed the glasses to Uncle, who said to me, 'Good night, my boy.' The first woman said, 'May God bless you', and the other woman bowed and smiled. Then van Rensburg and I went down in the lift to the basement, and got into his car.

'I told you I'd take you to the station,' he said. 'I'd take you home, but I'm frightened of Orlando at night.'

We drove up Eloff Street, and he said, 'Did you know what I meant?' I knew that he wanted an answer to something, and I wanted to answer him, but I couldn't, because I didn't know what that something was. He couldn't be talking about being frightened of Orlando at night, because what more could one mean than just that?

'By what?' I asked.

'You know,' he said, 'about our land being beautiful?'

Yes, I knew what he meant, and I knew that for God's sake he wanted to touch me too and he couldn't; for his eyes had been blinded by years in the dark. And I thought it was a pity, for if men never touch each other, they'll hurt each other one day. And it was a pity he was blind, and couldn't touch me, for black men don't touch white men any more; only by accident, when they make something like 'Mother and Child'.

He said to me, 'What are you thinking?'

I said, 'Many things', and my inarticulateness distressed me, for I knew he wanted something from me. I felt him fall back, angry, hurt, despairing, I didn't know. He stopped at the main entrance to the station, but I didn't tell him I couldn't go in there. I got out and said to him, 'Thank you for the sociable evening.'

'They liked having you,' he said. 'Did you see that they did?'

I said, 'Yes, I saw that they did.'

He sat slumped in his seat, like a man with a burden of incomprehensible, insoluble grief. I wanted to touch him, but I was thinking about the train. He said good-night, and I said it too. We each saluted the other. What he was thinking, God knows, but I was thinking he was like a man trying to run a race in iron shoes, and not understanding why he cannot move.

When I got back to Orlando, I told my wife the story, and she wept.

The Park

JAMES MATTHEWS 1974

Matthews was born in Cape Town in 1929. One of the problems of growing up as a young coloured boy in Cape Town must have been an inability to understand why you were not allowed to share in the most ordinary of things which most of us would take for granted, like playing in a park or swimming on a beach. This story evokes through a small boy's eyes the puzzlement, frustration and anger that this causes, and it makes us vividly aware of the pettiness as well as the larger injustices of the system of apartheid.

He looked longingly at the children on the other side of the railings: the children sliding down the chute, landing with feet astride on the bouncy lawn; screaming as they almost touched the sky with each upward curve of their swings; shrieking their demented joy at each dip of the merry-go-round. He looked at them and his body trembled and ached to share their joy. Next to him, on the ground, was a bundle of clothing, washed and ironed, wrapped in a sheet.

Five small boys, pursued by two bigger ones, ran past, ignoring him. One of the bigger boys stopped. 'What are you looking at, you brown ape?' the boy said, stooping to pick up a lump of clay. He recognised him. The boy had been present the day he was put out of the park. The boy pitched the lump, shattering it on the rail above his head, and the fragments fell on his face.

He spat out the particles of clay clinging to the lining of his lips, eyes searching for an object to throw at the boys separated from him by the railings. More boys joined the one in front of him and he was frightened by their number.

Without a word he shook his bundle free of clay, raised it to his head and walked away.

As he walked he recalled his last visit to the park. Without hesitation he had gone through the gates and got on to the nearest swing. Even now he could feel that pleasurable thrill that travelled the length of his body as he rocketed himself higher, higher, until he felt that the swing would up-end him when it reached its peak. Almost leisurely he had allowed it to come to a halt

like a pendulum shortening its stroke, and then he had run towards the
see-saw. A white boy, about his own age, was seated opposite him.
Accordion-like their legs folded and unfolded in turn to send the see-saw
jerking from the indentations it pounded in the grass. A hand pressed on his
shoulder. He turned around to look into the face of the attendant.

'Get off!'

The skin tightened between his eyes. Why must I get off? What have I done?
He held on, hands clamped on to the iron bar attached to the wooden
see-saw. The white boy jumped off from the other end and stood there, a
detached spectator.

'You must get off!' The attendant spoke in a low voice so that it would not
carry to the people who were gathering. 'The council say,' he continued, 'that
us blacks don't use the same swings as the whites. You must use the swings
where you stay.' His voice apologised for the uniform he wore, which gave
him the right to watch over little white boys and girls and ensure they were
not hurt while playing.

'There no park where I stay.' He waved a hand in the direction of a block of
flats. 'Park on the other side of town but I don't know where.' He walked past
them. The mothers with their babies, pink and belching, cradled in their
arms, the children lolling on the grass, his companion from the see-saw, the
nurse girls – their uniforms their badge of indemnity – pushing prams. Beside
him walked the attendant.

The attendant pointed an accusing finger at a notice-board near the
entrance. 'There. You can read for yourself.' Absolving himself from all
blame.

He struggled with the red letters on the white background. 'Blankes Alleen.
Whites Only.' He walked through the gates and behind him the swings
screeched, the see-saw rattled, and the merry-go-round rumbled.

He walked past the park each time he delivered the washing, eyes wistfully
taking in the scene.

He shifted the bundle to a more comfortable position, easing the pain
biting into his shoulder muscles. What harm would I be doing if I were to use
the swings? Would it stop the swings from swinging? Would the chute
collapse? The bundle pressed deeper and the pain became an even line across
his shoulders, and he had no answer to his reasoning.

The park itself, with its wide lawns and flower beds and rockeries and
dwarf trees, meant nothing to him. It was the gaily painted red-and-green

tubing, the silver chains and brown boards, his transport to never-never land, which gripped him.

Only once, long ago, and then almost as if by mistake, had he played on something to beat it. He had been taken by his father, one of the rare times he was taken anywhere, to a fairground. He had stood captivated by the wooden horses with their gilded reins and scarlet saddles dipping in time to the music as they whirled by.

For a brief moment he was astride one. He prayed it would last for ever, but the moment lasted only the time it took him to whisper the prayer. Then he was standing clutching his father's trousers, watching the others astride the dipping horses.

Another shift of the bundle and he was at the house where he delivered the clothing his mother had washed in a round tub filled with boiling water, the steam covering her face with a film of sweat. Her voice, when she spoke, was as soft and clinging as the steam enveloping her.

He pushed the gate open and walked around the back, watching for the aged lap-dog which at his entry would rush out to wheeze asthmatically around his feet and nip with blunt teeth at his ankles.

A round-faced African girl, her blackness heightened by the white starched uniform she wore, opened the kitchen door to let him in. She cleared the table and he placed the bundle on it.

'I call madam,' she said, the words spaced and highly-pitched as if she had some difficulty in uttering the syllables in English. Her buttocks bounced beneath the tight uniform and the backs of her calves shone with fat.

'Are you sure you've brought everything?' was the greeting he received each time he brought the bundle, and each time she checked every item and as usual nothing was missing. He looked at her and lowered his eyes as he said, 'Everything there, merrum.'

What followed had become a routine between the three of them.

'Have you had anything to eat?' she asked him.

He shook his head.

'Well, we can't let you go off like that.' Turning to the African woman in the white, starched uniform. 'What have we got?'

The maid swung open the refrigerator door and took out a plate of food. She placed it on the table and set a glass of milk next to it.

The white woman left the kitchen when he was seated and he was alone with the maid. His nervousness left him and he could concentrate on what was on the plate. A handful of peas, a dab of mashed potatoes, a tomato sliced into bleeding circles, a sprinkling of grated carrot, and no rice. White people are funny, he told himself. How can anyone fill himself with this? It doesn't form a lump like the food my mama makes. He washed it down with milk.

'Thank you, Annie,' he said as he pushed the glass aside. He sat fidgeting, impatient to be outside, away from the kitchen with its glossy, tiled floor and steel cupboards ducoed a clinical white to match the food-stacked refrigerator.

'I see you've finished.' The voice startled him. She held out an envelope containing the rand note – payment for his mother's weekly struggle over the wash-tub. 'This is for you.' A five-cent piece was dropped into his hand, a long fingernail raking his palm.

'Thank you, merrum.' His voice hardly audible.

'Tell your mother I'm going away on holiday for about a month and I'll let her know when I'm back.'

Then he was dismissed and her heels tapped out of the kitchen.

He nodded his head at the African maid who took an apple from a bowl bursting with fruit and handed it to him. He grinned his thanks and her responding smile bathed her face in light. He walked down the path finishing the apple with big bites.

The dog was after him before he reached the gate, its hot breath warming his heels. He turned and poked his toes into its face. It barked hoarsely in protest, a look of outrage on its face. He laughed delightedly at the expression which changed the dog's features into those of an old man.

'Let's see you do that again.' He waved his feet in front of the pug's nose. The nose retreated and made an about-turn, waddling away with its dignity deflated by his affront.

As he walked, he mentally spent his five cents. I'll buy a penny drops, the sour ones that taste like limes, penny bull's-eyes, a packet of sherbet with the licorice tube at the end of the packet, and a penny star toffees, red ones that turn your spit into blood.

His glands were titillated and his mouth filled with saliva. He stopped at the first shop and walked in.

Trays were filled with expensive chocolates and sweets of a type never seen in the jars on the shelves of the Indian shop on the corner where he stayed. He walked out without buying a thing.

His footsteps lagged as he reached the park. The nurse girls with their babies and prams were gone, their places occupied by old men who, with their hands holding up their stomachs, cast disapproving eyes over the confusion and clatter confronting them.

A ball was kicked perilously close to an old man, and the boy who ran after it stopped short as the old man raised his stick, daring him to come closer.

The rest of them called to the boy to get the ball. He edged closer and made a grab at it as the old man swung his cane. The cane missed the boy by more than a foot and he swaggered back, the ball held under his arm. Their game was resumed.

He watched them from the other side of the railings – the boys kicking the ball, the children cavorting on the grass, even the old men, senile on the seats; but most of all, he watched the children enjoying themselves with what was denied him, and his whole body yearned again to be part of them.

'Shit it!' He looked over his shoulder to see if anyone had heard him. 'Shit it!' he said louder. 'Shit it! Shit it!'

His small hands impotently shook the tall railings towering above his head. It struck him that he would not be seeing the park for a whole month, that there would be no reason for him to pass it. Despair filled him. He had to do something to ease his anger. A bag filled with fruit peels was on top of the rubbish stacked in a waste basket fitted to a pole. He reached for it, threw it over the railings, and ran without waiting to see the result.

Out of breath three streets further, he slowed down, pain stabbing beneath his heart. The act had brought no relief, only intensified the longing. He was oblivious of the people passing, the hoots of the vehicles whose paths he crossed without thinking. And once, when he was roughly pushed aside, he did not even bother to look and see who had done it.

The familiar shrieks and smells told him that he was home. Even the Indian shop could not draw him out of his melancholy mood and he walked past it, his five-cent piece unspent in his pocket.

A group of boys were playing with tyres on the pavement. They called him but he ignored them and turned into a short side-street. He mounted the flat stoep of a two-storey house with a façade that must once have been painted but had now turned a nondescript grey with the red brick underneath showing.

Beyond the threshold the room was dim. He walked past the scattered furniture with a familiarity that would have guided him blindfolded.

His mother was in the kitchen hovering over a pot perched on a pressure stove. He placed the envelope on the table. She put aside the spoon and stuck a finger under the flap of the envelope, tearing it in half. She placed the rand note in a spoutless teapot on the shelf.

'You hungry?'

He nodded his head. She poured him a cup of soup and added a thick slice of brown bread. Between bites of bread and sips of soup which scalded his throat, he told his mother that there would not be any washing coming during the week.

'Why? What the matter? What I do?'

'Nothing. Merrum say she go away for month. She let mama know she back.'

'What I do now?' Her voice took on a whine and her eyes strayed to the teapot containing the money. The whine hardened to reproach as she continued. 'Why don't she let me know she going away then I can look for another merrum?' She paused. 'I slave away and the pain never leave my back but it too much for her to let me know she go away. The money I get from her keep us nice and steady. How I go cover the hole?'

He wondered how the rand note he had brought helped to keep them nicely steady. There was no change in their meals. It was, as usual, not enough, and the only time they received new clothes was at Christmas.

'I must pay the burial, and I was going to tell Mr Lemonsky to bring lino for the front room. I'm sick looking at the lino full of holes but I can forget now. With no money you got as much hope as getting wine on Sunday.'

He hurried his eating to get away from her words before they could soak into him, trapping him in the chair as the witness to his mother's miseries.

Outside, they were still playing with their tyres. He joined them half-heartedly. As he rolled the tyre his spirit was still in the park, on the swings. There was no barrier to his coming and he could do as he pleased. He was away from narrow streets and squawking children and speeding cars. He was in a place of green grass and red tubing and silver steel. The tyre rolled past him. He made no effort to grab it.

'Get the tyre!' 'You sleep?' 'Don't you want to play any more?'

He walked away, ignoring their cries.

Rage boiled up inside him. Rage against the houses with streaked walls and smashed panes, filled by too many people; against the overflowing garbage pails outside doors; the alleys and streets; and against a law he could not understand – a law that shut him out of the park.

He burst into tears. He swept his arms across his cheeks to check his weeping, then lowered his hands to peer at the boy confronting him.

'I think you cry!'

'Who say I cry? Something in my eye and I rub it.'

He pushed past and continued towards the shop. 'Cry baby!' the boy's taunt rang after him.

The shop's sole iron-barred window was crowded. Oranges were mixed with writing paper and dried figs were strewn on school slates. Clothing and crockery gathered dust. Across the window a cockroach made its leisurely way, antennae on the alert.

Inside, the shop was as crowded as the window. Bags covered the floor, leaving a narrow path to the till. The shopkeeper, an ancient Indian with a face tanned like cracked leather, leaned across the counter. 'Yes, boy?' He showed teeth scarlet with betel-nut. 'Come'n, boy. What you want? No stand here all day.' His jaws worked at the nut held captive by his stained teeth.

He ordered penny portions of his selections, transferred the sweets to his pockets, threw the torn wrappings on the floor, and walked out. Behind him the Indian murmured grimly, jaws working faster.

One side of the street was in shadow. He sat with his back against the wall, savouring the last of the sun. Bull's-eye, peppermint, a piece of licorice – all lumped together in his cheek. For a moment the park was forgotten. He watched without interest the girl advancing.

'Mama say you must come'n eat.' She stared at his bulging cheek, one hand rubbing the side of her nose. 'Gimme.' He gave her a bull's-eye which she dropped into her mouth between dabs at her nose.

'Wipe your snot!' he ordered her, showing his superiority. He walked past. She followed, sucking and sniffing. Their father was already seated at the table when they entered the kitchen.

'Must I always send somebody after you?' his mother asked.

He slipped into his seat and then hurriedly got up to wash his hands before his mother could find fault on another point. Supper was a silent affair except for the scraping of spoons across plates and an occasional sniff from his sister.

A thought came to his mind almost at the end of the meal. He sat, spoon poised in the air, shaken by its magnitude. Why not go to the park after dark? After it had closed its gates on the old men, the children, and the nurses with their prams! There would be no one to stop him.

He could think no further. He was light-headed with the thought of it. His mother's voice, as she related her day to his father, was not the steam that stung, but a soft breeze wafting past him, leaving him undisturbed. Then qualms troubled him. He had never been in that part of town at night. A band of fear tightened across his chest, contracting his insides, making it hard for him to swallow his food. He gripped his spoon tightly, stretching his skin across his knuckles.

I'll do it! I'll go to the park as soon as we're finished eating. He controlled himself with difficulty. He swallowed what was left on his plate and furtively watched to see how the others were faring. Hurry up! Hurry up!

He hastily cleared the table when his father pushed the last plate aside, and began washing up. Each piece of crockery was passed for drying to his sister whose sniffing kept pace with their combined operation.

The dishes done, he swept the kitchen and carried out the garbage bin.

'Can I go play, mama?'

'Don't let me have to send for you again.'

His father remained silent, buried behind the newspaper.

'Before you go,' – his mother stopped him – 'light the lamp and hang it in the passage.'

He filled the lamp with paraffin, turned up the wick and lit it. The light glimmered weakly through the streaked glass.

The moon, to him, was a fluorescent ball – light without warmth – and the stars were fragments chipped off it. Beneath street lights card games were in session. He sniffed the nostril-prickling smell of dagga as he walked past. Dim doorways could not conceal couples clutching at each other.

Once clear of the district, he broke into a trot. He did not slacken his pace as he passed through the downtown area with its wonderland shop windows. His elation seeped out as he neared the park and his footsteps dragged.

In front of him was the park with its gate and iron railings. Behind the railings, impaled, was the notice-board. He could see the swings beyond. The sight strengthened him. He walked over, his breath coming faster. There was no one in sight. A car turned a corner and came towards him, and he started at the sound of its engine. The car swept past, the tyres softly licking the asphalt.

The railings were icy-cold to his touch and the shock sent him into action. He extended his arms and with monkey-like movements pulled himself up to perch on top of the railings, then dropped onto the newly turned earth.

The grass was damp with dew and he swept his feet across it. Then he ran, the wet grass bowing beneath his bare feet. He ran towards the swings, the merry-go-round, the see-saw, the chute, his hands covering the metal.

Up the steps to the top of the chute. He stood outlined against the sky. He was a bird; an eagle. He flung himself down on his stomach, sliding swiftly. Wheeeeeee! He rolled over when he slammed onto the grass. He looked at the moon for an instant then propelled himself to his feet and ran for the steps of the chute to recapture that feeling of flight. Each time he swept down the chute, he wanted the trip never to end. He wanted to go on sliding, sliding, sliding.

He walked reluctantly past the see-saw, consoling himself with a push at one end to send it whacking down on the grass.

'Shit it!' he grunted as he strained to set the merry-go-round into action. Thigh tensed, leg stretched, he pushed. The merry-go-round moved. He increased his exertions and jumped on, one leg trailing at the ready to shove if it should slow down. The merry-go-round dipped and swayed. To keep it moving, he had to push more than he rode. Not wanting to spoil his pleasure, he jumped off and raced for the swings.

Feet astride, hands clutching silver chains, he jerked his body to gain momentum. He crouched like a runner then violently straightened. The swing widened its arc. It swept higher, higher, higher. It reached the sky. He could touch the moon. He plucked a star to pin to his breast. The earth was far below. No bird could fly as he. Upwards and onwards he went.

A light switched on in the hut at the far side of the park. It was a small patch of yellow on a dark square. The door opened and he saw a figure in the doorway. Then the door was shut and the figure strode towards him. He knew it was the attendant. A torch glinted brightly as it swung at his side.

He continued swinging.

The attendant came to a halt in front of him, out of reach of the swing's arc, and flashed his torch. The light caught him in mid-air.

'God dammit!' the attendant swore. 'I told you before you can't get on the swings.'

The rattle of the chains when the boy shifted his feet was the only answer he received.

'Why you come back?'

'The swings. I come back for the swings.'

The attendant catalogued the things denied them because of their colour. Even his job depended on their goodwill.

'Blerry whites! They get everything!'

All his feelings urged him to leave the boy alone, to let him continue to enjoy himself, but the fear that someone might see them hardened him.

'Get off! Go home!' he screamed, his voice harsh, his anger directed at the system that drove him against his own. 'If you don't get off, I go for the police. You know what they do to you.'

The swing raced back and forth.

The attendant turned and hurried towards the gate.

'Mama, Mama!' His lips trembled, wishing himself safe in his mother's kitchen, sitting next to the still-burning stove with a comic spread across his knees. 'Mama. Mama!' His voice mounted, wrenched from his throat, keeping pace with the soaring swing as it climbed the sky. Voice and swing. Swing and voice. Higher. Higher. Higher. Until they were one.

At the entrance of the park the notice-board stood tall, its shadow elongated, pointing towards him.

The Truth, Mama

MOTHROBI MUTLOATSE 1980

Growing up in a racially divided South Africa must have been a difficult thing for young children to understand, as is shown in this story. It shows the human tragedy present in very ordinary and recognisable families as a result of government legislation, in this case the Bantu Education Act, which required that Black students in their first schools must receive instruction in their own language. This was opposed by the Blacks and liberal thinkers as it was important to give them access to English rather than leaving them ghettoised. How in this story can Ma-Nthato ('Mama') begin to explain 'the truth' to her waiting children?

'Where will we be going to this Christmas, Mama?' That was chubby, six-year-old, inquisitive Busisiwe, interrupting her mother as she wrapped up her provisions for someone special. Somebody very dear and yet so far, from the Serowe family of six . . . its head.

The father of Busi, five-year-old Nthato, seventeen-year-old Matimba and nineteen-year-old Xoli.

The husband of Morongwe. Phuthuma . . .

All Ma-Nthato – as she was affectionately known in the neighbourhood of Jabavu because of Nthato's pranks and antics – could mumble, was something like: 'There's no need to go anywhere this year.'

Back came Busi's question: 'Why, Mama?'

Ma-Nthato frowned: 'Oh . . . because there's nowhere we can go to this time.'

Xoli, the eldest of the children and a high school student at Morris Isaacson – before the State took over forty schools, that is – looked up from the copy of *Ebony* he was absorbed in, and challenged his mother. Not so gently, though:

'Mama, why can't you tell her the truth?'

'I can't as yet, Xoli, and you know it.'

'Know what, Mama?' Busi queried further.

Just then, Matimba, who'd come in from attending one of the ghetto educational courses at the Early Learning Centre (Entokozweni) in Molet-sane, intervened:

'What is going on in here, Ma?'

Xoli intercepted: 'She's selling Busi, here, a dummy.'

'Watch your language, Xoli. Very soon you will be sorry,' Ma-Nthato chided him.

But Xoli was not to be discouraged easily. Politely, he told his sister, Matimba, an ex-student at Naledi High (ex, again, because of the legalised hijacking of her school): 'Mama is playing a game of hide and seek with Busi. She refuses to tell her why we won't be going out this Christmas.'

Suddenly Ma-Nthato, to avoid an intense cross-examination by Xoli, and possibly Matimba, announced that the children would have to excuse her there and then. She had to leave for Modder Bee Prison.

Slip of the tongue: prison.

This was the first time in three weeks, since the disappearance of her husband – a few days after what was being referred to as the 'crack-down' – that she had mentioned the word 'prison' in the presence of all the children, though both Matimba and Xoli, as the elder children, had visited their father twice.

Ma-Nthato had decided, much against Xoli's protestations, not to tell the smaller children where their father was.

'How long, mother, do you think that you can hide the truth from them? And do you think it is wise?' Xoli had asked then.

All this returned in a flash to her, as well as to Xoli, when she slipped up by referring to Modder Bee Prison by name.

Each time she left with *umphako* and kisses for everyone (except Xoli who argued that kisses were reserved for his girl-friend only), Ma-Nthato would innocently but deliberately lie that she was visiting Ntate – the children's father – at his place of employment!

But now *nta etswile pepeneneng*. The cat was out of the bag!

For all to see – and diagnose clinically. As well as ethically.

Xoli took advantage of the situation and went on the encitement path.

'There's no way in which you can duck this one, Ma. You will have to tell them the truth. The whole, absolute truth – before they learn it from awkward quarters.'

'Will you stop harassing me,' Ma-Nthato protested, trying hard to conceal her embarrassment. She momentarily stole a glance at the expressions on all her children's faces to assess the situation.

When she saw and, in a way, smelled the curiosity, the unquenched curiosity in them, she decided to tell the truth. And let nature take its course.

But the difficult part was, how to tell it without losing face at the same time for having delayed the truth so long. And yet, there was no valid reason for doing so in the circumstances. Or was there?

She realised then that she would have to tell the truth in a skilful manner – to appease Xoli for instance, though she doubted that Xoli would ever be satisfied with anything less than his father's release.

The silence that ensued was trying. And piercing.

'We're still awaiting your explanation, Ma,' Matimba reminded her, disturbing Ma-Nthato's day-dreaming.

'Here's a chair, Mama,' Xoli said, matter-of-factly.

Busi, who had been quiet all along, opened the home inquisition with the obvious. 'What are you going to do at Modder Bee – isn't it a jail where criminals are kept? Like we were told by our teacher in Sunday School?'

Ma-Nthato heaved a sigh – she was near a mental breakdown as she sat down – with her children encircling her as they would their granny when she taught them history the human way each time they visited her.

'Where do I begin?' Ma-Nthato asked.

'You begin from the beginning,' retorted Xoli.

'Naturally,' added Matimba.

The smaller children were amused by this style of dialogue.

'Ma,' Xoli continued, 'simply tell them where Baba is, why he is there, and how long he anticipates being there. Don't make a short story long. Simply give them the facts. It is much better that they hear this news from no one but you. They are certainly going to be more relieved than shocked. That's my own opinion, though.'

Matimba appealed to her mother to speak the truth 'and it shall set you free'.

Naïve as it may seem, the last remark by Matimba acted as a catalyst to Ma-Nthato. At least, she thought to herself, they are asking for an explanation from me because they dearly miss their father!

'Well children . . . the truth is,' she heard herself say, not believing that the words were really coming, 'your father is, in fact, at Modder Bee Prison.'

'And so he's a criminal,' Busi let go.

'No, he's not actually.'

'And so what is he doing there?' Nthato asked sharply.

'This is going to be a hell of a "court case",' Ma-Nthato mumbled to herself.

'What was that, Mama?' Matimba jumped in.

'Nothing, really, I was speaking to myself . . .'

'Is Mama sick then?' Busi wanted to know.

Xoli, who had been listening with arms folded as if he was the judge, explained: 'Mama is not sick . . . she's only concerned . . .'

Ma-Nthato did not know whether Xoli was being sarcastic or extra-sweet.

'Your father is not a criminal,' said Ma-Nthato quietly.

'If he's not a criminal what is he then? A worker at Modder Bee?'

'He does not work there,' Xoli put in. 'You know, as well as everybody does, that he was a teacher – until he resigned in protest against this monster that is Bantu Education, together with more than three hundred other teachers.'

Ma-Nthato took the cue: 'Your father was detained– '

Busi flashed back: 'What do you mean, "detained"?'

'Can you explain that for me, Xoli?' Ma-Nthato appealed.

'Unfortunately, Ma, this is not the right time and place for me to do so.'

'Aw, I see,' replied Ma-Nthato.

Was there a hint of sarcasm?

Nthato joined the bandwagon: 'Why was Ntate detained, Ma?'

Busi was not to be beaten to the punch: 'You wait your turn, Nthato: I was the one who was doing the asking. I want to know the meaning of "detained".'

'Children, can't we postpone this until I come back?'

'Noo!' was the chorus.

'The truth, Mama . . . Tell the truth here and now,' said Xoli, sort of matter-of-fact.

To start the ball rolling, he began humming, quietly, the ghetto hymn, 'Senzeni Na?'

And, this time, Ma-Nthato was left with no alternative but to get the whole damned thing off her shoulders. Before the children unleashed real thunderbolts!

'Baba was detained – the police took him to Modder Bee under the Internal Security Act.'

'And what is that?' Busi enquired, with a worried expression.

Ma-Nthato looked at Xoli, but there was no sign of help ever coming from that end. So she essayed a lay person's interpretation of the law: 'It's a law under which people are arrested for politics.'

Like a fox-terrier, Busi shot back: 'And what is politics?'

'It is a long, long story.'

'Please tell us about it, Ma.' That was Matimba – of all people!

'Politics is saying something the Government doesn't like.'

'Who is this Govern-what?' Nthato chipped in.

'The Government are people who control this land.'

'What did Baba say that they didn't like?'

'Nthato, you sure ask too many questions . . .'

'But Ma, they have taken Baba away – what for, we don't know. What did Baba tell them that they didn't like?'

'He said, among other things, that he won't teach under Bantu Education any more.'

Busi got in before she was squeezed out again: 'But that is what we Ama-Azanians are fighting against. Everybody hates Bantu Education because all it produces is tear-gas.'

Matimba also wanted to know from her mother what the other reasons were for their father's detention.

Painstakingly, Ma-Nthato answered: 'I think it was because he said the Black man was well qualified enough now to run the Black man's affairs. Oh, children, you are torturing me.'

Even Xoli was touched.

He asked: 'Did Baba actually say so, Mama?'

'Y-y-yes,' sobbed Ma-Nthato. 'And he may be held for up to a year . . . that's why we cannot go away this Christmas, Busi.'

The tiny delicate creature, no, angel, was really moved.

'Mama, do you know what?'

'N-no, Busi.'

'I'm proud of my father . . . and of you too. Despite all the trouble we give every day before you leave for work in town, you still love us.'

'Care for us,' added Xoli as he slowly ambled towards his mother, arms outstretched.

'Christmas is no longer a time of enjoyment for us,' said Matimba in a soft tone. 'All our people have been detained.'

'All we can do is abstain from all pleasures – and remember all those who have been detained. And, like Biko, have died in detention.'

'Mother,' Xoli said as he embraced his tear-filled mother, 'I love you with all my heart. Forgive me for undermining you – for thinking poorly of you. I didn't know, I just didn't know how much all this was hurting you.'

Ma-Nthato smiled a little at Xoli and said: 'Your father would be proud of you now. In fact, he would have been disappointed if you had behaved otherwise. And were it not for your tough talk, I myself would have suffered a nervous breakdown long ago.'

In some surprise, Xoli found himself sobbing on his weeping mother. And the girls couldn't hold back their tears.

But then these were tears of togetherness. The family that would not allow detention to disrupt its unity.

Nor dampen its spirits.

The Man from the Board

RICHARD RIVE 1983

Richard Rive was a writer of great power and significance. His many stories and poems range across an extraordinary number of themes and moods. Born in 1931, he was what was known as a 'Cape Coloured', that is, a person from the Cape Town area of mixed racial origins. Like Bosman earlier in this volume, therefore, he is writing here about his own people and this story is almost certainly based on his own experience. It shows with wry humour the petty bureaucracy which the system of apartheid needed to enable it to function. Rive's writing here contrasts with the violence that was sometimes characteristic of his work but its effectiveness in its demolition of the system is no less powerful for this.

Saturday afternoon in late January. A dull, monotonous, hot and sweaty Saturday afternoon when the knock came at the door of his flat. Rather louder than usual. Isaac sat listlessly at his desk, listless and a trifle irritated at the unexpected interference with his boredom. Three review books for which he had no stomach. The inevitable file of Method assignments for correction. Bored and irritated. A hot Saturday afternoon with nothing he wanted to do. The noon edition of the *Argus* lay half-read, crumpled on the floor. A student's essay lay open on his desk. A dull student's dull essay. Give a detailed analysis of the aims of teaching Oral in the primary school. He wiped a drop of sweat out of his eyes and stared lethargically at the page of scrawled, infantile handwriting. Watch television maybe. Sports. Mediocre club matches, show-jumping, squash. Get into the car and drive anywhere. Why? Where? Where do people always drive to on Saturday afternoons in the heat? Strandfontein? Kalk Bay? Sports meetings? The country? Everyone seems so purposeful, hurrying to so clearly defined a destination. Somewhere definite like out in the country.

The knock came again, louder and slightly more purposeful than the first time.

Cars full of people driving out into the country. A sweaty man with sunglasses, his wife with sunglasses, and a rear-seat full of children and dogs.

All looking alike. One can tell the parents by the sunglasses. All determined to get wherever they are determined to get to. And then the stream of returning traffic. Always at six o'clock. Long six-o'clock queues of cars with the same people, the same dogs, the same dogged determination.

The knock again.

Isaac got up, annoyed but a trifle relieved at the temporary respite from boredom. He opened the door slowly, letting in a gust of hot air. He expected to find a hawker or a char looking for work. Instead he found a genial, red, sweaty face grinning at him.

'Yes? What do you want?'

'Are you Mr Jacobs? Mr Isaac Jacobs?'

He took in the figure, straining his eyes against the sunlight. A somewhat dumpy, middle-aged man. A dumpy little man wearing a khaki safari suit. Short, flabby knees, bow legs and long khaki stockings with a black comb stuck in the left one against the calf. What was it Graham had told him? Mike Graham had been with him at Cambridge, and while walking across the lawns of King's had remarked that if a man wore a safari suit with a comb in his sock he was a South African. But if he had no comb in his sock he was an Australian and almost sure to be called Neil. All Australians who wore safari suits were called Neil. Graham had made it sound like a great truth.

'Excuse me?' The safari suit opened an official-looking briefcase and extracted a cardboard file bursting with papers. He extracted one and ran his finger down a column. 'Jacobs, Isaac Vernon?'

'Yes, that's me.'

'Sounds Jewish. Ikey Jacobs. You sure you're not Jewish?' His eyes twinkled. 'After all, Sammy Davis Junior is Jewish.'

Isaac did not find this amusing by any means. It was hot standing in the doorway. Small beads of sweat formed just below his visitor's highly oiled hairline.

'May I come in? The heat's killing me.'

'Well, I suppose so. Yes, come inside. But what is it you want?' Isaac felt sure that somewhere his visitor had a Volkswagen Beetle to match his safari suit. A Beetle with a radio and a long aerial with an imitation orange stuck on the tip.

'Actually I'm from the Board.' He did not say which Board. 'Bredenkamp's the name. Mr Johannes Bredenkamp.'

Isaac wasn't sure exactly how his visitor had got inside, but while talking

Bredenkamp must have nudged his way past, for the next thing he was sinking down on the couch in the book-filled lounge. He took out an initialled handkerchief and mopped his brow a trifle ostentatiously.

'Nice and cool in here.'

Isaac knew it wasn't, but realised that Bredenkamp was determined to make conversation. His annoyance had changed to curiosity. Who was this man? What Board was he from? He seemed to take over the place, to fill the lounge with himself and his handkerchief. Crowding the place with his familiarity.

'Hard work this, working on a hot Saturday afternoon.' A pause. Isaac did not know how to respond.

'The Board has tried to contact you on many occasions, Mr . . .'

'Jacobs.'

'Mr Jacobs. Didn't you get our circular requesting an interview in our office? We sent the first few by post and then I came myself. I left one here two weeks ago. I put it in your letter-box. Didn't you get it?'

It now made sense. So this was the confrontation. He realised that he had to keep calm. So this was J. M. Bredenkamp whose signature had been below the cyclostyled letter, printed in both official languages on cheap paper, one line of Afrikaans immediately above the translated line in English. Dear Occupier. You are requested to see Mr J. M. Bredenkamp at an address . . . he could not remember. Somewhere in Plein or Barrack Street. Bring along your Identity Card or Book of Life. A request not an order. So he had ignored it. Come and tell Mr J. M. Bredenkamp your race classification. Dear Occupier, what the hell are you doing in the wrong Group Area? Come and show Mr Bredenkamp whether you are qualified or not.

'Did you receive any of our letters?' Bredenkamp's tone was not unpleasant.

'Yes, I received them.' His admission sounded flat. Why admit any more and proffer excuses? 'Yes, I got your letters.'

'Then why didn't you come and see us?' There was still no malice. In fact Bredenkamp clucked as if reprimanding a naughty child.

'Look, Mister. I have a job of work to do. I have students to worry about. I can't just take off every time someone sends me a circular.'

'But this is different. This is from the Board.'

'So what the hell.'

'Mr Jacobs. You realise you are living in a white area.'

'Yes?'

'By law you are not allowed to live here. It's illegal.'

'Because you people choose to label me coloured?'

'I don't make the laws, Mr Jacobs.' Bredenkamp could make a cliché sound even more like a cliché. 'I understand exactly how you feel but it's not my business. I'm not responsible for the law. We are only trying to help people like you, Mr Jacobs.'

Isaac felt the anger mounting again, but the heat militated against his working up enough enthusiasm. Should he not squash this petty little Napoleon? Hold him responsible? Wipe the grin off his face? The effort would be too much. Or would it?

'We are trying to help you, Mr Jacobs.'

'Really? In what way, may I ask?'

'Look at it this way. Wouldn't you be much happier living among your own people?'

Bredenkamp fairly beamed at his solicitousness.

'Now look here . . .'

'Mr Bredenkamp's the name.'

'Mr Bredenkamp. Who the hell do you think my people are?'

If the official was aware of any subtlety in the question, any nuance, he showed no sign of it.

'Who the hell are my people?' Isaac repeated.

'The coloured people,' Bredenkamp replied promptly.

'Hell. So you've decided to declare me coloured.'

'But you are. Aren't you?' Bredenkamp seemed genuinely puzzled at his attitude.

'All right, let's leave it at that for the moment. Now let me ask you a question. Do you sleep well at night?'

'Beg yours?'

'Do you sleep well at night after going around putting people out of their homes?'

'Oh, I see,' he beamed, 'I see what you are getting at. You are accusing the Board of putting you out of your flat. Do you really believe that, Mr Jacobs?'

'Indeed I do.'

'Why do you people always go around accusing us wrongly? Why do you people hate us so? – treat us as if we were Communists or terrorists or such things? We are here to help people like you.'

'And you do this by trying to put me out of my flat?'

'Nobody's putting you out. We must obey the law.'

'What the hell are you doing here?'

'We are here, Mr Jacobs, I say again, we are here to satisfy people, to help them, to protect them.'

'Do I look as if I need your protection?'

'Now come, come, Mr Jacobs. You must be reasonable. Similar people must stay together. Would you like any old skollie to live next door to you?'

Isaac was thrown off his guard for the moment. What exactly did he mean? Was there more in it? Was Bredenkamp hinting that by being in a white area he was the interloper, the skollie? Or was the official genuinely solicitous about who his neighbours should be? Was he as genial and naïve as he pretended to be? Why did he remain so friendly even under provocation? Should he not have jackbooted his way in, barked out a command and demanded that the occupier leave the area or face instant arrest? This man who must have some power (or was he a very petty clerk?) sat and beamed and swallowed insults. Was this the opening gambit of a more serious game? Was Bredenkamp deliberately confusing him? Getting him off his guard? Softening him up?

'What exactly do you mean about skollies living next door to me?'

'I mean what I say. Would you like simply anyone to live next door to you? Any old ruffian? I would certainly object if any white skollie had to come to live next door to me.'

'Mr Bredenkamp, I would object to any skollie as my neighbour – whether he is white or black. I insist on the right to choose my neighbours for myself. For instance I might very well object to your living next door to me.'

Either Bredenkamp was unaware of the innuendo or chose to ignore it. He did not for a moment lose his composure. Only his left hand in which he kept his crumpled handkerchief kept straying from his brilliantined hair to his brow.

'You don't really mean that, do you?' he asked at last. So he had understood. The barb had driven home.

'No, I don't,' Isaac found himself apologising. 'No, I don't. I'm sorry. But for goodness sake, Mister, come to the point. What do you want?'

'Anything cool. Have you a fizzy drink or something? Coke or orange will do. Otherwise just a glass of cold water, please.'

This deflated Isaac. Was this calculated effrontery, or just sheer ignorance?

Or was it a skilful avoidance of unpleasantness? He fetched a glass of orange juice from the fridge in the tiny kitchen. 'Sorry, I've run out of Coca-Cola.' He must be careful not to appear too friendly. Apologising for his remarks and for the fact that he had no Coke. Surely he was at the receiving end? Bredenkamp was there to put him out of his flat. Since when does the victim apologise to the tormentor? This was all wrong.

The official took long sips of the drink, between which he made pleasant clucking noises with his tongue. Then he carefully balanced the half-empty glass on the coffee table and took up his file.

'If you don't mind, now for a little business. Won't keep you long, Mr Jacobs.'

'Yes.'

'Mind if I ask a few routine questions?'

'Just go ahead.'

'Your full name is Isaac Vernon Jacobs?'

'Surely you know that?'

'Race – coloured.'

Isaac made no reply.

'Date of birth? Age? Address?'

'Tell me for the umpteenth time. What the hell is this in aid of?'

'Only routine questions, Mr Jacobs, just routine. You don't need to reply if you don't wish to. Job? I suppose you're a teacher or a lecturer.'

'Go ahead.'

'Where do you teach? University of the Western Cape?' He arched his brows knowingly. Isaac felt glad that Bredenkamp was very wrong but did nothing to disillusion him. Caution. The questions would obviously become less routine, more incriminating. Bredenkamp was no fool. Or was he? The official scribbled almost feverishly. What the hell was he writing?

'Tell me, how did you guess that I was a lecturer at Western Cape?'

'Easy. I can tell by all those books on your shelves.'

Could anyone be really so naïve, or was this a very clever act?

'So, if a black man has shelves full of books he must of necessity be a lecturer at Western Cape?'

'Of course.' Bredenkamp added with a note of finality. 'Besides you're not black, you're brown.'

'Oh, hell. All right, go ahead. Tell me more about myself since you seem to know everything.'

'You are obviously a bachelor.'

'Spot on. Now how on earth did you know that?' Isaac larded the remarks with heavy sarcasm.

'All those books on your shelves. I told you before.'

'I see. Yes indeed. I see. So I am a bachelor because I have books on my shelves. All lecturers at Western Cape are bachelors!'

'I never said that, Mr Jacobs. Besides, I like a man who reads a lot. I'm not a bachelor myself but I like reading. I'm married. Wife and two boys. Johan is seven and Niklaas five. I like my reading. Patience Strong and Zane Grey. You like Patience Strong?'

'Sure. Yes, sure I do.'

'And Zane Grey?'

'And Zane Grey.'

'Lucky you, being a bachelor and spending most of your time just lecturing and reading.'

'I would be far luckier, very much luckier and happier, were you to leave me alone to read in my own flat. Why do you want to put me out of here?'

Bredenkamp looked at him reproachfully. 'Now really, Mr Jacobs. I told you before that all we are trying to do is to help you. I'm here for instance to check on Indian businesses in this area. This is a white area. Indians aren't allowed to have businesses here. It's against the law.'

'Then why on earth do you have to come to me? Do I look like an Indian business?'

'I know you're not an Indian, Mr Jacobs, you're coloured.'

'Oh, hell, not again. If you are seaching for Indian businesses, or any other business for that matter, why come to me? Why send me your circulars? Does this flat look like a business to you? Do you find slippers under a bed in a business? Or pots on the stove? Or a television set?'

'I must say you've got a nice set, Mr Jacobs. Sony, isn't it? You prefer it?'

'What!'

'You prefer a Sony? I'm thinking about getting one for the boys. I like the colour but my wife is worried about the small screen. Do you find it too small?'

The conversation was becoming Kafkaesque and leading nowhere. Going round in circles. Becoming bizarre.

'Mr Bredenkamp, please listen to me. Could you please finish your questions and leave as soon as possible?'

'Now, now, Mr Jacobs. I'm sorry if I said anything to upset you. I was only talking about the Sony. I'm sorry to take up your time. I also have to earn my living. I really can't understand what you people can have against us.'

'I really haven't the time nor the inclination to go into that now. Is there anything else, Mr Bredenkamp? Anything more?'

'Yes, just the last detail. I can come back for the others some other time. What is your annual income? I hope you don't mind my asking?' He sounded apologetic.

'Must I answer that?'

'Not if you don't wish to.'

'Then I don't wish to.'

Bredenkamp nevertheless seemed to write down an answer. He did some rapid calculations, pursing his lips, then looked up, satisfied. Was he really writing down figures, or information for his superiors? For higher consideration?

'No children, of course. Unmarried. You lucky bachelor. You people have all the luck.'

Was there a veiled irony in the remark?

Bredenkamp looked Isaac full in the face. It was coming. 'Can I ask you a very important question? It's got nothing to do with the Board.' So this was it. This was the showdown.

'Yes?' Isaac braced himself for it.

'What is your philosophy of life?'

Now what the hell did that mean? 'Look here, Mister. I've no time for games. If you have relevant questions, ask them.'

'This is no game. I'm serious, Mr Jacobs.' He looked it.

'All right, Mr Bredenkamp. If I have what you call a philosophy of life, that is my personal affair.'

'I know I upset you. I'm sorry. I only ask because I can see from your books that you are a man of education. A man of philosophy. I have two books on philosophy at home. Above my bed. I try to read before I go to sleep but seldom have the time. I'm always busy as you can understand, Mr Jacobs.'

'Checking up on Indian businesses?'

'Come, come, Mr Jacobs. You know you're not an Indian.'

'Neither am I a bloody business.'

Mr Bredenkamp's smile remained but began to look a trifle frayed. Isaac rose to his feet in a manner which made it quite clear that the interview was over.

Bredenkamp sat for a moment, then rose reluctantly.

'Well. That's all for now, Mr Jacobs. You'll be hearing from us soon.' He gave no indication whether this was a threat or not. 'And thanks for the drink. It was very nice of you.' He nudged Isaac playfully in the ribs. 'And stick to a Sony. The colour is OK.'

Again Isaac's anger mounted. He steered the official to the door. How did you react towards a man who kept grinning at you? As he opened the door, there was a blast of heat. Bredenkamp stuck out his hand and Isaac reluctantly accepted.

''Bye for now. We'll be in contact, Mr Jacobs. I enjoy talking to intellectuals like you. We must have a long chat one day. Next time I come I'll bring my philosophy books with me.'

It seemed as if he was never going to release Isaac's hand. At length he did.

'Now where did I park my Volksie?'

This was irresistible. Isaac broke into a wide grin for the first time.

'You have a Volksie, Mr Bredenkamp?'

The official nodded while mopping.

'I thought so,' said Isaac as he shut his door.

The Prisoner Wore Glasses

BESSIE HEAD 1986

Bessie Head was another writer of mixed ('coloured') race, born in Pietermaritzburg in 1937, of an illegitimate union between a Scots mother and an African father. This caused such scandal that her mother's family succeeded in getting her certified insane, so that by the time Bessie was born her mother was in a mental hospital. She is another writer who quickly became known outside her own country. This tale has much in common with stories of prison camps in the Second World War. It shows how goodwill and good humour can survive in the most unlikely of circumstances.

Scarcely a breath of wind disturbed the stillness of the day and the long rows of cabbages were bright green in the sunlight. Large white clouds drifted slowly across the deep blue sky. Now and then they obscured the sun and caused a chill on the backs of the prisoners who had to work all day long in the cabbage field. This trick the clouds were playing with the sun eventually caused one of the prisoners who wore glasses to stop work, straighten up and peer short-sightedly at them. He was a thin little fellow with a hollowed-out chest and comic knobbly knees. He also had a lot of fanciful ideas because he smiled at the clouds.

'Perhaps they want me to send a message to the children,' he thought, tenderly, noting that the clouds were drifting in the direction of his home some hundred miles away. But before he could frame the message, the warder in charge of his work span shouted: 'Hey, what you tink you're doing, Brille?'

The prisoner swung round, blinking rapidly, yet at the same time sizing up the enemy. He was a new warder, named Jacobus Stephanus Hannetjie. His eyes were the colour of the sky but they were frightening. A simple, primitive, brutal soul gazed out of them. The prisoner bent down quickly and a message was quietly passed down the line: 'We're in for trouble this time, comrades.'

'Why?' rippled back up the line.

'Because he's not human,' the reply rippled down and yet only the crunching of the spades as they turned over the earth disturbed the stillness.

This particular work span was known as Span One. It was composed of ten men and they were all political prisoners. They were grouped together for convenience as it was one of the prison regulations that no black warder should be in charge of a political prisoner lest this prisoner convert him to the views. It never seemed to occur to the authorities that this very reasoning was the strength of Span One and a clue to the strange terror they aroused in the warders. As political prisoners they were unlike the other prisoners in the sense that they felt no guilt nor were they outcasts of society. All guilty men instinctively cower, which was why it was the kind of prison where men got knocked out cold with a blow at the back of the head from an iron bar. Up until the arrival of Warder Hannetjie, no warder had dared beat any member of Span One and no warder had lasted more than a week with them. The battle was entirely psychological. Span One was assertive and it was beyond the scope of white warders to handle assertive black men. Thus, Span One had got out of control. They were the best thieves and liars in the camp. They lived all day on raw cabbages. They chatted and smoked tobacco. And since they moved, thought and acted as one, they had perfected every technique of group concealment.

Trouble began that very day between Span One and Warder Hannetjie. It was because of the short-sightedness of Brille. That was the nickname he was given in prison and is the Afrikaans word for someone who wears glasses. Brille could never judge the approach of the prison gates and on several previous occasions he had munched on cabbages and dropped them almost at the feet of the warder and all previous warders had overlooked this. Not so Warder Hannetjie.

'Who dropped that cabbage?' he thundered.

Brille stepped out of line.

'I did,' he said meekly.

'All right,' said Hannetjie. 'The whole Span goes three meals off.'

'But I told you I did it,' Brille protested.

The blood rushed to Warder Hannetjie's face.

'Look 'ere,' he said. 'I don't take orders from a kaffir. I don't know what kind of kaffir you tink you are. Why don't you say Baas. I'm your Baas. Why don't you say Baas, hey?'

Brille blinked his eyes rapidly but by contrast his voice was strangely calm.

'I'm twenty years older than you,' he said. It was the first thing that came to mind but the comrades seemed to think it a huge joke. A titter swept up the line. The next thing Warder Hannetjie whipped out a knobkerrie and gave

Brille several blows about the head. What surprised his comrades was the speed with which Brille had removed his glasses or else they would have been smashed to pieces on the ground.

That evening in the cell Brille was very apologetic.

'I'm sorry, comrades,' he said. 'I've put you into a hell of a mess.'

'Never mind, brother,' they said. 'What happens to one of us, happens to all.'

'I'll try to make up for it, comrades,' he said. 'I'll steal something so that you don't go hungry.'

Privately, Brille was very philosophical about his head wounds. It was the first time an act of violence had been perpetrated against him but he had long been a witness of extreme, almost unbelievable human brutality. He had twelve children and his mind travelled back that evening through the sixteen years of bedlam in which he had lived. It had all happened in a small, drab little three-bedroomed house in a small, drab little street in the Eastern Cape and the children kept coming year after year because neither he nor Martha ever managed the contraceptives the right way and a teacher's salary never allowed moving to a bigger house and he was always taking exams to improve his salary only to have it all eaten up by hungry mouths. Everything was pretty horrible, especially the way the children fought. They'd get hold of each other's heads and give them a good bashing against the wall. Martha gave up something along the line so they worked out a thing between them. The bashings, biting and blood were to operate in full swing until he came home. He was to be the bogey-man and when it worked he never failed to have a sense of godhead at the way in which his presence could change savages into fairly reasonable human beings.

Yet somehow it was this chaos and mismanagement at the centre of his life that drove him into politics. It was really an ordered, beautiful world with just a few basic slogans to learn along with the rights of mankind. At one stage, before things became very bad, there were conferences to attend, all very far away from home.

'Let's face it,' he thought ruefully. 'I'm only learning right now what it means to be a politician. All this while I've been running away from Martha and the kids.'

And the pain in his head brought a hard lump to his throat. That was what the children did to each other daily and Martha wasn't managing and if Warder Hannetjie had not interrupted him that morning he would have sent the following message: 'Be good comrades, my children. Co-operate, then life will run smoothly.'

The next day Warder Hannetjie caught this old man of twelve children stealing grapes from the farm shed. They were an enormous quantity of grapes in a ten gallon tin and for this misdeed the old man spent a week in the isolation cell. In fact, Span One as a whole was in constant trouble. Warder Hannetjie seemed to have eyes at the back of his head. He uncovered the trick about the cabbages, how they were split in two with the spade and immediately covered with earth and then unearthed again and eaten with split-second timing. He found out how tobacco smoke was beaten into the ground and he found out how conversations were whispered down the wind.

For about two weeks Span One lived in acute misery. The cabbages, tobacco and conversations had been the pivot of jail life to them. Then one evening they noticed that their good old comrade who wore the glasses was looking rather pleased with himself. He pulled out a four ounce packet of tobacco by way of explanation and the comrades fell upon it with great greed. Brille merely smiled. After all, he was the father of many children. But when the last shred had disappeared, it occurred to the comrades that they ought to be puzzled. Someone said: 'I say, brother. We're watched like hawks these days. Where did you get the tobacco?'

'Hannetjie gave it to me,' said Brille.

There was a long silence. Into it dropped a quiet bombshell.

'I saw Hannetjie in the shed today,' and the failing eyesight blinked rapidly. 'I caught him in the act of stealing five bags of fertiliser and he bribed me to keep my mouth shut.'

There was another long silence.

'Prison is an evil life,' Brille continued, apparently discussing some irrelevant matter. 'It makes a man contemplate all kinds of evil deeds.'

He held out his hand and closed it.

'You know, comrades,' he said. 'I've got Hannetjie. I'll betray him tomorrow.'

Everyone began talking at once.

'Forget it, brother. You'll get shot.'

Brille laughed.

'I won't,' he said. 'That is what I mean about evil. I am a father of children and I saw today that Hannetjie is just a child and stupidly truthful. I'm going to punish him severely because we need a good warder.'

The following day, with Brille as witness, Hannetjie confessed to the theft of the fertiliser and was fined a large sum of money. From then on Span One did very much as they pleased while Warder Hannetjie stood by and said nothing. But it was Brille who carried this to extremes. One day, at the close of work Warder Hannetjie said: 'Brille, pick up my jacket and carry it back to the camp.'

'But nothing in the regulations says I'm your servant, Hannetjie,' Brille replied coolly.

'I've told you not to call me Hannetjie. You must say Baas,' but Warder Hannetjie's voice lacked conviction. In turn, Brille squinted up at him.

'I'll tell you something about this Baas business, Hannetjie,' he said. 'One of these days we are going to run the country. You are going to clean my car. Now, I have a fifteen-year-old son and I'd die of shame if you had to tell him that I ever called you Baas.'

Warder Hannetjie went red in the face and picked up his coat.

On another occasion Brille was seen to be walking about the prison yard, openly smoking tobacco. On being taken before the prison commander he claimed to have received the tobacco from Warder Hannetjie. All throughout the tirade from his chief, Warder Hannetjie failed to defend himself but his nerve broke completely. He called Brille to one side.

'Brille,' he said. 'This thing between you and me must end. You may not know it but I have a wife and children and you're driving me to suicide.'

'Why don't you like your own medicine, Hannetjie?' Brille asked quietly.

'I can give you anything you want,' Warder Hannetjie said in desperation.

'It's not only me but the whole of Span One,' said Brille, cunningly. 'The whole of Span One wants something from you.'

Warder Hannetjie brightened with relief.

'I think I can manage if it's tobacco you want,' he said.

Brille looked at him, for the first time struck with pity, and guilt.

He wondered if he had carried the whole business too far. The man was really a child.

'It's not tobacco we want, but you,' he said. 'We want you on our side. We want a good warder because without a good warder we won't be able to manage the long stretch ahead.'

Warder Hannetjie interpreted this request in his own fashion and his interpretation of what was good and human often left the prisoners of Span One speechless with surprise. He had a way of slipping off his revolver and picking up a spade and digging alongside Span One. He had a way of producing unheard-of luxuries like boiled eggs from his farm nearby and things like cigarettes, and Span One responded nobly and got the reputation of being the best work span in the camp. And it wasn't only take from their side. They were awfully good at stealing certain commodities like fertiliser which were needed on the farm of Warder Hannetjie.

Standing here, and I'm unable to go out and help the injured, is driving me mad.'

'Where are the children?' She asked anxiously.

'They joined the march this morning. I never saw them after that.'

'Oh God, please bring them home safe. It is terrible out there and all we can do is just sit here while our children are fighting the whole army and all those guns. I feel so helpless, Amos.'

'I feel exactly the same, Miriam. I wish I had died in that accident!'

'Oh Amos, my husband. Why do you talk like that? Soon you will be strong and on your feet again. We must not give in now. Our children need our support. Come, let's see what there is to eat. What you need is a nice cup of tea.'

'Don't worry, my wife. You go and look for the boys. I can get something to eat for myself. Besides, I feel like being alone.'

'Why do you want to be alone? I've just come in from work to be with you, and you want to be alone?'

'I know your heart is out there with the boys. You go and look for them. I'll be all right.'

'Are you sure, Amos?' she asked tenderly.

She went to the kitchen to drink some water as her throat was irritated by the gas. She noticed that the boys had left in a great hurry – plates of half-eaten mealie meal still stood on the table. The large enamelled basin was filled with dirty dishes and the bucket that Fassie used to scrub the floor stood under the old wooden kitchen table. They had never before left for school before cleaning the house, but that morning was obviously an exception. She went back into the bedroom to tell Amos that she was leaving. As she turned away Amos looked sadly at her, thinking, 'We live in such dangerous times that you don't know if you'll see your loved ones again once they leave the house. Bloody murderers!'

Miriam reached the gate and then turned quickly back into the house. She stood in the doorway and shouted, 'Are you sure you're all right? Don't leave the house until I return. Do you hear me, Amos?'

'Go, Wife, go! But take care. These people are out to kill us today.'

She rushed out into the street. Stones rained from behind walls and bushes. She had to dodge and run to avoid the missiles. There were tyres burning in the streets, barricading the way of the Casspirs. But the iron monsters moved forward relentlessly. The faces of the men on the Casspirs, she noticed, were red with anger. Thick palls of tear-smoke filled the air and the tyres gave off acrid fumes which inflamed the eyes and throat. She heard gunshots in the next street and the piercing cries of the children. It was like a nightmare as she made her way to her sister's home a few streets away. She found herself running with the crowd at times. Perhaps her sons were at their Aunt Susan's home, hiding?

As she entered Susan's home she immediately felt that something was amiss. She found her in the kitchen shaking in a panic. Holding her ten-month-old baby over the kitchen sink she was blowing air into the child's mouth. This beautiful child with her large brown eyes, who was always gurgling with delight, now lay limp in her mother's arms!

'What happened?' Miriam asked, very alarmed.

'They threw a tear-gas canister through the doorway. Little Dolly had just crawled there to sit in the sun,' answered Susan, tears running down her cheeks. 'My baby almost choked to death.'

'Give her to me,' said Miriam, and she held the child to her body. Slowly she rocked Dolly while her sister wiped the little face with a wet, cold face-cloth.

'I'm looking for Steve and Fassie. They didn't attend school today but joined the march. I thought they may be here with you, Sister.'

'I didn't see them today, Miriam. Where can they be? Perhaps they're hiding someplace.'

'But I want to find them before I go back to my work this evening.'

'Are you off today?'

'I decided to come home when I heard the news of the beatings on the radio.'

'Why didn't they allow this peaceful march?' Susan asked angrily.

'Yes, they want to shoot all of us,' answered Miriam. 'Here, I think she's sleeping.' Miriam handed Dolly back to Susan. 'You must watch her, anything can happen. I must leave now and search for the boys. Keep your door closed,' she warned as she left.

Back on the streets she followed the crowd. By now her heavy body felt tired and sweaty. She ran along searching the crowd for her sons' faces amongst them. They were all singing freedom songs but nowhere did she see Steve or Fassie. The faces of the youths shocked her. She detected signs of hope, determination and defiance in them. On the way she met many mothers and stopped to talk to some of them that she knew.

'I'm looking for my sons,' she tried to explain. They ignored her in their rush to get away.

'No time to talk,' said one of the young men in the crowd.

'Come on, Mama. If you stand too long in one place they will shoot you,' said another.

She joined the others, half-running and half-walking. Passing another woman she asked, 'Are you also looking for your children?'

'Yes, yes!' several of the mothers in the crowd answered in great apprehension.

'Not one of them are at school today.'

'They say that they are doing what we should have done years ago.'

'That's true,' approved several women.

When she approached her street she said goodbye to them and returned home very disappointed.

'Miriam, Miriam. Is it you?' Amos called from the bedroom. 'Did you find them?'

'Oh, Amos. You'll never believe what's going on out there! It seems that all the high school students joined the march this morning. I tell you Amos, these children don't care about their lives!' She was now so overcome that she just sat down on the bed, crying.

'All right, Mother. Don't worry! It will turn out all right. I know it,' he pacified her.

'I will not go back to work until I've found my sons,' she said between her tears.

'What if you lose your job?'

'We will manage on Winnie's money. We've been through worse times before. But I'm going to stay here where I belong. Let the rich do their own work for a change. I'm tired of cooking, cleaning and picking up after them. I hate them all! They couldn't care a damn about us.'

'My wife, you've been running around since this morning,' said Amos, looking at her with great concern. 'Come, let me make that cup of tea we were going to have this morning.' He shuffled into the kitchen followed by Miriam.

'You must rest that leg of yours. Let me make the tea instead and I'll tell you what is going on out there. The children are all over the township. The roads are blocked with old mattresses and oil drums. I saw some of them making petrol bombs behind a wall. I can't believe it! There is a war going on out there, Amos.'

'And no sign of our sons? I'm sure they will come home soon.'

'Want some more tea?' she asked him. They continued to discuss the situation until late in the afternoon.

Suddenly the front door burst open and about six young people stormed inside breathlessly, seeking a place to hide. With them was Steve. When he saw his mother he was visibly surprised.

'Mama, why are you home from your work?'

'How can I stay at work with all this happening here?'

All Steve's friends seemed extremely nervous and fearful and cast anxious looks towards the front door.

'We must hide in here. Away from the police, Ma! They're after us and they are going to kill us, Ma!'

'Kill? Not while I'm around.'

Amos suggested that two should hide behind the toilet in the back yard. They ran outside as fast as they could. Miriam pushed two boys into the bedroom. Steve and the last one jumped into the old fireplace which was covered by an old floral curtain. When they were safely in their hiding places, Miriam poked her head behind the curtain. 'Where is your brother, Fassie?'

'I don't know. Shuh! Please go away, Mama. We'll go and look for him later. Please go, Ma.' She returned to Amos and they stared at each other as a deathly silence fell over the house.

A loud crash preceded the front door being kicked open and in marched several policemen. They went straight into the kitchen without any invitation. Miriam's heart beat so fast that she could feel the colour warming her face, her hair soaked in sweat. Amos pretended that he was reading a book. It looked as if a blue-grey cloud of uniforms and hateful brown, black and red faces had invaded Miriam's kitchen. They confronted her and Amos with their guns at the ready. Miriam said a silent prayer.

'Where are they?' demanded the leader. 'We saw them come in this house,' he shouted at the two old people. His men backed him in unison.

'You saw wrong,' Miriam shouted back in the same tone, surprising even Amos with her courage. 'There is no one in this house but myself and my husband. How do you know they came here? All these council houses look the same.'

'Search the whole place! And outside in the yard,' the big red bull bellowed to his men.

They kicked over the dustbin in the yard. They threw everything around with absolute contempt. The men inside were deliberately knocking over chairs and one officer ripped the curtains from the windows, declaring, 'This bloody house is as dark as hell!' Others went kicking open the inside doors of the house, searching everywhere. One even turned over the old zinc bath which the family used for their weekly bath. He flung it to the cement floor so that it made the sound of a bomb going off in the room. They appeared to be pleased with the chaos they were causing. But they did not discover any of the children! One of the policemen returned: 'There is only that old stink shithouse out there.'

'Where are they?' the sergeant shouted at Amos in anger and pulled at his crutch. Amos almost fell and a sharp pain shot up his bad leg. Miriam quickly held on to him.

'We don't know. We are alone here, my Baas,' he whimpered.

On hearing the word 'Baas' the sergeant looked pleased, thinking that he was in control of the situation. He called his men and ordered them to stop the search. The house was a shambles when they marched out. 'We will be back,' shouted the sergeant over his shoulder.

As a parting gift one of the policemen threw a tear-gas canister into the kitchen. Miriam and Amos struggled towards the bedroom to save themselves from choking. After shutting the bedroom door behind them they fell down onto the bed, bewildered. Every room in the house was soon filled with tear-smoke. Miriam had grabbed a wet face-cloth from behind the bedroom door and held it over Amos's face as he had seemed to faint. Quickly she opened the bedroom window. 'They are pigs. Just smell this house! Are you all right?' she asked Amos.

'We must live like this because we are of the wrong colour, Mother.'

One by one the boys crept out of their hiding-places and thanked Miriam and Amos politely, almost apologetically, for the trouble they had caused. Miriam ordered them to open all the windows and doors to get the smell out of the house. 'It's our duty to protect you children,' said Miriam.

The children discussed the events of the day in the back room where Steve and Fassie slept. In their bedroom Miriam and Amos sat in silence. Finally she asked, 'Where is our Fassie?'

'I hope he is safe,' answered Amos. She started to weep softly. After a while she knelt down to pray at his side. Amos tenderly laid his hand on her while the young people continued their meeting. Their loud and angry voices filtered through to the bedroom.

'I saw them baton-charge a young girl as she lay on the ground.'

'That policeman hit her over the body with the strength of an ox!' said Steve.

'I saw them whip a priest full in the face, shattering his spectacles. I'm sure he's lost the sight in that eye. I've never seen anything so cruel,' said another.

'What about the two old nuns they arrested!' someone complained angrily.

'All our leaders have been detained. Tomorrow we will meet at school and decide how to protest against this injustice,' said Steve.

'One of you go outside and see if the police vans are still patrolling. We must search for my brother. We must find him!'

As they prepared to leave, their look-out returned to whisper, 'It's all clear. They've left the area.'

On the way out Steve went into his parents' room. His father was asleep but his mother was sitting next to him, just staring into space. 'We are going to look for Fassie, Ma. You rest now, I can see that you are tired.'

'God go with you, Son.' She lay down next to her husband, but she was awake for a long time still. In the distance she heard the sound of gunshots, and people running and screaming.

The following morning she awoke with a headache and her body felt stiff all over. Quietly she tiptoed into the next room to see if Steve had returned home the previous night. On seeing the sleeping figure she murmured, 'Thank God.' Miriam shook him awake, asking softly, 'Do you have any news about your brother?'

'We've looked all over, Ma. But he cannot be found.'

Miriam went silently into the kitchen to cook a pot of mealie meal for breakfast. As she stirred the porridge she decided to go to Groote Schuur Hospital to tell Winnie about Fassie's disappearance.

'Maybe she can help,' she said to herself. After they had had their breakfast Steve prepared to leave for school.

'I'm going to Winnie for help. Maybe Fassie is in hospital,' Miriam stated.

'Take care how you walk, Ma. Don't take chances out there,' said Steve. 'I'm off now. 'Bye Ma and Pa. Take care now,' he shouted on his way out.

'I must be off too,' Miriam said to Amos.

'Will you be all right or shall I come with you?'

'Now how can you come with your injured leg? No, you stay here. I won't be long.' She pulled a scarf over her head, kissed him and left the house with feelings of anticipation that she would somehow find Fassie.

The streets were scattered with stones and the burnt-out tyres had left imprinted circles on the asphalt roads from the previous day's unrest. As she passed the high school she saw massive army trucks parked outside the grounds with police and soldiers patrolling inside the fence. Their rifles were hanging down their sides. A helicopter hovered overhead. A Buffel troop-carrier appeared from around a corner like an angry buffalo with a cannon for a nose, ready to attack. The township looked like a battlefield and a deathly atmosphere pervaded the scene which seemed to expect more violence. She hurried on and when she arrived at the hospital she climbed the stairs to Ward T2 where Winnie was on duty. They embraced each other.

'You look terrible, Ma. Are Steve and Fassie okay?' Winnie asked anxiously.

'That's why I'm here. They joined the march to Pollsmoor yesterday. Now Fassie is missing. We are sick with worry.'

'Wait, let me ask Matron for a few minutes off, then we can talk inside.'

After a short while Winnie returned and took her mother's arm. They went through the male wards of the hospital. Winnie searched among the faces of the patients for her brother's, but without success.

'Come, let's go to the out-patients, Ma,' suggested Winnie. They found the corridors crowded with injured people from the townships. Inside the hall the benches were packed, and the doctors were busy attending to some people with gunshot wounds. A young boy howled for his mother. Winnie and Miriam walked amongst the injured people searching for Fassie but he was not to be found there.

Winnie saw her mother out, kissed her and promised to change her shift and come home as soon as possible. Miriam walked to the bus stop as if in a trance. After she had paid her fare, she counted the money in her purse. As there wasn't enough left for her to go straight home, she decided to collect her wages at the big house. However, to her surprise Steve was waiting for her at the Claremont bus terminus. Her heart started racing as he came towards her.

'What is it, Son?' she asked apprehensively.

'Fassie is on the run, Ma,' he blurted out.

'Why, what happened?' she asked. 'What does it mean?'

'He threw a petrol bomb at a police van. They saw his face and gave chase. He hid in someone's house and then jumped the fences. They followed him. If they find him he will go to jail. They know who he is! We will just have to wait for him to return home when the time is right.'

'I thank the Lord, he is alive. When will this unrest end?' she cried.

'No one knows. Looks like it's only started.' Steve looked grim-faced.

'Look, Steve, I have no more money. We need food. I'm going to Madam to explain the situation to her. She will understand and give me my money. I'll go back to work when Fassie comes home. Now I must go to the big house. Are you coming with me, Steve?'

'No, Ma. I don't like it amongst those people. You go. I'll go home to Pa. But please bring some food home, Ma.'

They each went their own way, she back to Paradise Road and Steve back to the township.

As she opened the gate of her employer's home, the dog ran to meet her. She went around to the back door and in the yard, to her surprise, she met a new maid with a bucket and rags hanging from her arm.

'Is the Madam home?'

'Yes. She is drinking her tea on the patio,' the girl answered shyly.

Miriam walked through the huge house to the poolside. There she saw Madam sunbathing. She went closer. 'Good afternoon, Madam,' she said in a shaking voice. She didn't know how to go on.

Madam looked up and replied casually, 'Oh, you finally arrived, Miriam.'

In a defiant mood Miriam replied, 'I've had a lot of trouble, Madam. My son is gone. My Fassie is missing!'

'I believe there is unrest in all the townships. Why are you people so violent? And where is your son? He is supposed to be at school, not so?'

'I see someone has already taken my place. Why the hurry?'

'Well, you let me down badly, Miriam. I had no alternative – if you can run home whenever you hear a gunshot sound in the township! Master and I have decided that it would be best if you stay home. Now let me pay you your month's wages. I have decided to deduct from your money the cost of the figurine you smashed. Is that okay, Miriam?'

'Yes, Madam. And my reference? I will have to look for other work. My husband is sick at home as you know,' Miriam pleaded softly.

'I shall post your papers, or you can tell your new employer to phone me.' Madam went inside and soon returned with Miriam's wages. 'Now if you don't mind, Miriam, my tea is getting cold.'

Miriam walked away, her shoulders slumped. 'Now that is appreciation for all the work I have done here!' she thought.

She walked through the large kitchen, opened the refrigerator and helped herself to a cool drink. On the table she saw a tempting cream cake topped with red cherries – Master's favourite nightcap! She cut a slice, then another and another – she could not stop eating. When she had had her fill she cut another large slice and wrapped it up to take home to Amos. She picked all the cherries off the topping and stuffed them into her mouth. Finally, feeling satisfied, she went out into the back yard.

Suddenly she remembered that Madam had a bad habit of accusing her servants of stealing. She had a pen in her handbag and she went back to the kitchen. She took a piece of writing paper from the kitchen cupboard drawer and wrote a message to Madam. 'I ate the cake and enjoyed it, Madam.' She pushed the note into the cream of the leftover cake. On her way out she greeted the new maid. 'Poor girl,' she said to herself.

As she walked down the avenue she felt good – even a little happy. 'How foolish can one get! Why should I feel this way over a piece of cake?' she thought. The trees looked even greener than the day before. The bird-songs sounded louder and sweeter. She stopped to open her pay-packet to see how much Madam had taken for the figurine. Counting the money, she discovered that her carelessness had cost her ten rand. She swore to herself!

She decided that she must hurry home now, back to the gunshots and all the chaos. The avenue seemed longer today, or was it perhaps her tiredness? She stopped for a short rest, sitting on an old tree stump. A squirrel ran past her with an acorn in its mouth. As she admired the little creature which scrambled up a huge tree to feed its family, she remembered her family had eaten only mealie meal that morning. She would have to go to the shops on her way through Claremont. The loss of the ten rand for the figurine had set her back financially, but they would manage somehow. She must also buy the daily newspapers for Amos as he was an avid reader. And some fruit and a chocolate for each one! 'But what will I do with Fassie's bar? I will have to keep it until his return,' she said to herself and then, without expecting any answer, 'I wonder where my son is hiding now?'

Suddenly she felt sad as she pictured Amos alone all day, wobbling around on crutches in the small, dark council house. Miriam remembered that he had always bought her fruit and a chocolate bar on his pay-day. She got up from the old tree stump and continued down the road. At the bottom of the hill she turned back and could still see the big house in the distance. She wiped the sweat from her forehead and took one last look at Paradise Road.

Olifants River, Kruger National Park

Shadows

DAMON GALGUT 1988

Damon Galgut, who was born in Pretoria in 1963, is one of the new generation of White South African writers and published his first novel (*A Sinless Season*) at the age of 19. Although he has written about the politics of his country, he has mainly concerned himself with themes of friendship, love and family. This is increasingly the case with the younger generation of South African writers who can begin to build a literature out of more universal themes than the ones concerning the power struggle that has dominated so much earlier writing. In this story he deals with great delicacy with a difficult subject and the tale is typical of his insights into basic human feelings.

The two of us are pedalling down the road. The light of the moon makes shadows under the trees, through which we pass, going fast. Robert is a little ahead of me, standing up in his seat. On either side of his bike the dogs are running, Ben and Sheba, I can never tell the difference between them.

It's lovely to be like this, him and me, with the warm air going over us like hands.

'Oh,' I say. 'Oh, oh, oh . . .'

He turns, looking at me over his shoulder. 'What?' he calls.

I shake my head at him. He turns away.

As we ride, I can see the round shape of the moon as it appears between the trees. With the angle of the road it's off to the right, above the line of the slope. The sky around it is pale, as if it's been scrubbed too long. It hurts to look up.

It's that moon we're riding out to see. For two weeks now people have talked about nothing else. 'The eclipse,' they say. 'Are you going to watch the eclipse?' I didn't understand at first, but my father explained it to me. 'The shadow of the earth,' he says, 'thrown across the moon.' It's awesome to think of that, of the size of some shadows. When people ask me after this, I tell them, 'Yes,' I tell them, 'I'm going to watch the eclipse.'

But this is Robert's idea. A week ago he said to me, 'D'you want to go down to the lake on Saturday night? We can watch the eclipse from there.'

'Yes,' I said. 'We can do that.'

So we ride down towards the lake under the moon. On either side the dogs are running, making no sound in the heavy dust, their tongues trailing wetly from the corners of their mouths.

The road is beginning to slope down now as we come near to the lake. The ground on either side becomes higher, so that we're cycling down between two shoulders of land. The forest is on either side, not moving in the quiet air. It gives off a smell: thick and green. I breathe deeply, and my lungs are full of the raw, hairy scent of the jungle.

We're moving quite fast on the downhill, so we don't have to pedal any more. Ahead of me, I see Robert break from the cut in the road and emerge again into the flat path that runs across the floor of the forest. A moment later I do so too, whizzing into the heavy layers of shadows as if they are solid. The momentum is wonderful, full of danger, as if we're close to breaking free of gravity. But it only lasts a moment. Then we're slowing again, dragged back by the even surface of the road and the sand on the wheels.

The turn-off is here. I catch up with Robert and we turn off side by side, pedalling again to keep moving. Ahead of us the surface of the lake is between the trees, stretched out greenly in the dark. The trees thin out, there's a bare strip along the edge of the water.

We stop here. The path we were riding on goes, straight and even, into the water. That's because it used to lead somewhere before they flooded the valley to make the lake. They say that under the water there are houses and gardens, standing empty and silent in the currents below. I think of them and shiver. It's always night down there at the bottom of the lake; the moon never shines.

But we've stopped far from where the path disappears. We're still side by side, straddling the bikes, looking out. The dogs have also stopped, stock-still, as if they can smell something in the air. There's a faint wind coming in off the water, more of a breeze really. On the far side of the lake we can see the lights of houses. Far off to the right, at the furthest corner of the water, are the lights of my house. I glance towards it and try to imagine them: my father and mother, sitting out on the front verandah, looking across the water to us. But there are no lights where we are.

'There,' says Robert.

He's pointing. I follow his finger and I also see it: the moon, clear of the trees on the other side. It really is huge tonight, as if it's been swollen with water. If you stare at it for long enough you can make out the craters on its surface, faint and blue, like shadows. Its light comes down softly like rain and I see I was wrong – it makes the water silver, not green.

'We've got a view of it,' I say.

But Robert is moving away already. 'Come,' he says. 'Let's make a fire.'

We leave the bikes leaning together against the trunk of a tree and set out to look for firewood. We separate and walk out by ourselves into the forest. But I can still see Robert a little distance away as he wanders around, bending now and then to pick up bits of wood. The dogs are with him. It isn't dense or overgrown down here. The floor of the forest is smooth. Apart from the sound of our feet and the lapping of the lake, it's quiet here.

There isn't much dead wood around. I pick up a few branches, some chunks of log. I carry them down to where the bikes are. Robert has already made one trip here, I see from a small pile of twigs. I don't much feel like this hunting in the dark, so I delay a while, wiping my hands on my pants. I look out over the water again. I feel so calm and happy as I stand, as if the rest of my life will be made up of evenings like this. I hear Robert's whistling coming down to me out of the dark behind. It's a tune I almost recognise. I start to hum along.

As I do I can see Robert in my mind's eye, the way he must be. When he whistles, small creases appear round his lips. He has a look of severe concentration on his face. The image of him comes often to me in this way, even when I'm alone. Sometimes late at night as I lie trying to sleep, a shadow cast in from outside will move against the wall and then he breaks through me in a pang, quick and deep. We've been friends for years now, since I started high school. It's often as if I have no other friends. *He* has, though. I see him sometimes with other boys from the school, riding past my house in a swirling khaki pack down to the lake. It hurts me when this happens. I don't know what they speak about, whether they talk of things that I could understand. I wonder sometimes if they mention me. I wonder if they mock me when I'm not there and if Robert laughs at me with the rest of them.

He comes down now, carrying a load of wood in his arms. 'Is that all?' he says, looking at what I collected. 'What's the matter with you?'

'Nothing,' I say, and smile.

He drops his wood along with the rest and turns. He's grinning at me: a big skew grin, little bits of bark stuck to his hair and the front of his shirt.

'Do we need any more?'

'No,' he says. 'That should do fine.'

We build a fire. Rather – he builds the fire and I sit against a tree to watch. It always seems to be this way: him doing the work, me watching. But it's a comfortable arrangement, he doesn't mind. I like the way he moves. He's a skinny boy, Robert, his clothes are always slightly loose on him. Now as I watch, my eye is on his hands as they reach for the wood and stack it. His hands are slender and brown. He's brought a wad of newspaper on his bike. He twists rolls of paper into the openings between the logs.

Like me, the dogs are sitting still and watching. They stare at him with quiet attention, obedient and dumb.

He lights the fire. He holds the burning match and I'm looking for a moment at this white-haired boy with flame in his hand. Then he leans and touches it to the paper. Smoke. He shakes out the match.

The fire burns, the flames go up. In a minute or two there's a nice blaze going. We're making our own light to send across the water. I think of my parents on the wooden verandah, looking across to the spark that's started up in the darkness. They point. 'There,' they say. 'That's where they are.' I smile. The fire burns. The flames go up. The heat wraps over my face like a second skin. The dogs get up and move away, back into the dark where they shift restlessly, mewing like kittens.

In a little time the fire burns down to a heap of coals. They glow and pulse, sending up tiny spurts of flame. We only have to throw on a stick now and then. Sitting and staring into the ring of heat, it would be easy to be quiet but we talk, though our voices are soft.

'We should camp out here sometime,' he says. 'It's so still.'

'Yes,' I say. 'We should do that.'

'It's great to be away,' he says. 'From them.'

He's speaking of his family, his home. He often speaks of them this way. I don't know what he means by this: they all seem nice enough. They live in a huge, two-storeyed house made out of wood, about half an hour's ride from us. They're further up the valley, though, out of sight of the lake. There are five of them: Robert, his parents, his two brothers. I'm alone in my home, I have no brothers. Perhaps it's this that makes their house a beautiful place to me. Perhaps there really is something ugly in it that I haven't seen. Either way, we don't spend much time there. It's to my home that Robert likes to come in the afternoons when school is done. He's familiar to us all. He comes straight up to my room, I know the way he knocks on my door. Bang-bang, thud.

My mother has spoken to me about him. At least twice that I can remember she's sat on my bed, smiling at me and playing with her hands.

'But what's wrong with it?' I say. 'Everyone has friends.'

'But lots,' she says. 'Lots of friends. You do nothing else, you see no one else . . .'

'There's nothing else to do,' I say. 'Other people bore me.'

'There's sport,' she says. 'I've seen them at the school, every afternoon. Why don't you play sport like other boys? You're becoming thinner and thinner.'

It's true. I am. When I look at myself in the mirror I'm surprised at how thin I am. But I'm not unhealthy, my skin is dark, I'm fit. We ride for miles together, Robert and me, along the dust roads that go around the lake.

'It's him,' I say. 'Isn't it? It's him you don't like.'

'No,' she says. 'It isn't that. I like him well enough. It's you, you that's the matter.'

I don't want to upset them, my parents. I want to be a good son to them. But I don't know any way to be fatter than I am, to please them. I do my best.

'I'll try,' I say. 'I'll try to see less of him.'

But it doesn't help. Most afternoons I hear his knock at my door and I'm glad at the sound. We go out on our bikes. This happens at night too, from time to time. As now – when we find ourselves at the edge of the lake, staring at the moon.

'D'you want a smoke?' he says.

I don't answer. But he takes one out of the box anyway, leaning forward to light it in the fire. He puffs. Then he hands it to me. I take a drag, trying to be casual. But I've never felt as easy about it as Robert seems to. The smoke is rough in my throat, it makes my tongue go sour. I don't enjoy it. But for the sake of Robert I allow this exchange to take place, this wordless passing back and forth, this puffing in the dark. I touch his hand as I give it back to him.

'Are you bored?' he asks. 'Why're you so quiet?'

'No,' I say. 'I'm fine.' I think for a while, then ask, 'Are you?'

'No,' he says.

But I wonder if he is. In sudden alarm I think of the places he might rather be, the people he might rather be with. To confirm my fear, he mutters just then:

'Emma Brown– '

'Why are you thinking about Emma Brown?' I say. 'What made you think of her now?'

He's looking at me, surprised. He takes the cigarette out of his mouth. 'I was just wondering,' he says. 'I was just wondering where she is.'

'Why?' I say.

'I just wondered if she was also watching the moon.'

'Oh,' I say, and smile bitterly into the fire. I don't know what's going through his head, but mine is full of thoughts of her: of silly little Emma Brown, just a bit plump, with her brown hair and short white socks. I remember a few times lately that I've seen her talking to Robert; I remember him smiling at her as she came late to class.

'I was just thinking,' he says, and shrugs.

I finish the cigarette. I throw the butt into the fire. We don't talk for a long time after that. I can hear the dogs licking each other, the rasping noise of their tongues. I begin to feel sad. I think of my anger and something in me slides, as if my heart is displaced.

He reaches out a hand and grazes my arm. It's just a brief touch, a tingle of fingers, but it goes into me like a coal. 'Hey,' he says. 'What's the matter?'

'Nothing,' I say. 'Nothing.' I want to say more, but I don't like to lie. Instead I say again, 'Nothing.' I feel stupid.

The fire burns down to a red smear on the ground. Across the water the lights have started to go out. Only a few are left. I look off to the right: the lights in my house are still on. My parents keep watch.

When I look back, Robert is on his feet. His head is thrown back. I don't stand, but I gaze over his shoulder at what he's watching: the white disc of the moon, from which a piece has been broken. While we were talking, the great shadow of the earth has started to cover the moon. If you look hard enough, the dark piece can still be seen, but only in outline, as if it's been sketched with chalk.

We stare for a long time. As we do, the shadow creeps on perceptibly. You can actually see it move.

'Wow,' he says.

Sensing something, one of the dogs throws back its head in imitation of us and begins to howl. The noise goes up, wobbling on the air like smoke.

'Sheba,' says Robert. 'Be quiet.'

We watch the moon as it sinks slowly out of sight. Its light is still coming down, but more faintly than before. On the whole valley, lit weirdly in the strange blue glow, a kind of quiet has fallen. There is nothing to say. I lower my eyes and look out over the water. Robert sits down next to me on his heels, hugging his knees. 'You know,' he says, 'there's times when everything feels . . . feels . . .'

He doesn't finish.

'I know,' I say.

We sit and watch. Time goes by. The trees are behind us, black and big. I look across to my home again and see that the lights have gone out. All along the far shore there is dark. We're alone.

'It's taking a long time,' he says. 'Don't you think?'

'Yes,' I say. 'It is.'

It's hot. The dogs are panting like cattle in the gloom. I feel him along my arm. A warmth. I spring up, away. 'I'm going to swim,' I say, unbuttoning my shirt.

I take off my clothes, and drop them on the sand. The dogs are standing, staring at me. Robert also watches, still crouched on his heels, biting his arm. When I'm naked I turn my back on him and walk into the lake. I stop when the water reaches my knees and stand, arms folded across my chest, hands clinging to my ribs as if they don't belong to me. It isn't cold, but my skin goes tight as if it is. One of the dogs lets out a bark. I walk on, hands at my sides now, while the water gets higher and higher. When it reaches my hips I dive. It covers my head like a blanket. I come up, spluttering. 'It's warm,' I say, 'as blood.'

'Hold on,' he calls. 'I'm– '

As I turn he's already running. I catch a glimpse of his body, long and bright as a blade, before he also dives. When he comes up, next to me, the air is suddenly full of noise: the barking of the dogs as they run along the edge of the lake, the splashing of water, the shouts of our voices. It *is* our voices I hear, I'm surprised at the sound. I'm laughing. I'm calling out.

'Don't you,' I say, 'don't you try–'

We're pushing at each other, and pulling. Water flies. The bottom of the lake is slippery to my feet, I feel stones turn. I have hold of Robert's shoulder. I have a hand in his hair. I'm trying to push him under, wrenching at him while he does the same to me. He laughs.

Nothing like this has taken place between us before. I feel his skin against me, I feel the shape of his bones as we wrestle and lunge. We're touching each other. Then I slide, the water hits my face. I go under, pulling him with me, and for a moment we're tangled below the surface, leg to leg, neck to neck, furry with bubbles, as if we'll never pull free.

We come up together into quiet. The laughter has been doused. We still clutch to each other, but his fingers are hurting me. We stand, face to face.

While we were below, the last sliver of moon has been blotted out. A total dark has fallen on the valley, so that the trees are invisible against the sky. The moon is a faint red outline overhead. I can't see Robert's face, though I can feel his breath against my nose. We gasp for air. The only sound to be heard is the howling of the dogs that drifts in from the shore: an awful noise, bereaved and bestial.

I let go. And he lets go of me. Finger by finger, joint by joint, we release one another till we are standing, separate and safe, apart. I rub my arm where he hurt it.

'Sorry,' he mutters.

''S okay,' I say. 'It doesn't matter.'

After that we make our way to shore. I wade with heavy steps, as if through sand. By the time I reach the edge and am standing, dripping, beside my clothes, the moon has begun to emerge from shadow and a little light is falling. The dogs stop howling. I don't look up as I dress. I put my clothes on just so, over my wet body. They stick to me like mud.

I wait for him to finish dressing. As he ties his shoelaces I say, not even looking at him, 'What d'you think will happen?'

'What d'you mean?' he says.

'To us,' I say. 'D'you think in ten years from now we're even going to know each other?'

'I don't know what you mean,' he says.

He sounds irritated as he says this, as if I say a lot of things he doesn't understand. Maybe I do. I turn away and start to walk back to the bikes.

'Hey,' he calls. 'What you . . . don'tcha want another smoke or somethin' before we go?'

'No,' I say. 'Not me.'

I wait for him at the tree where the bikes are leaning. He takes his time. I watch him scoop water over the coals. They make a hissing noise, like an engine beneath the ground. Then he walks up towards me along the bank, hands in his pockets. The sight of him this way, sulking and slow, rings in me long after we've mounted our bikes and started back up the path.

By the time we rejoin the dust road a little way on, the soreness in me is smaller than it was. One of the dogs runs into his way and he swears. At this I even manage to laugh. I look off and up to the left, at the moon which is becoming rounder by the minute. Its light comes down in soft white flakes, settling on us coldly as we ride.

Head Work

ABEL PHELPS   1990

Abel Phelps arrived in South Africa from England at the age of 17 in 1927. In this story the whole of the absurdity of apartheid is turned upside-down by a clever trick. It is only with the possibilities of an emerging new South Africa that matters so serious can be turned into a joke, but Abel Phelps succeeds here in making us both laugh and think seriously at the same time.

When you have been in one job for seventeen years, ever since you left school, you think it will last until you die. You think of being out of work as something that happens to other people. You hear them talk down in the township. 'Fanie is out of work again,' they say. But when you hear the whole story, you hear that he turned up drunk for work in the morning and quarrelled with the boss, or that he put the wrong labels on the tins twice running, so that when the people opened fig it turned out apricot. Then you pat yourself on the back and say, 'It couldn't happen to me. I'm all right.' Another thing that made it safe was that our jam factory was part of a big group, they couldn't go bankrupt.

Then we heard a rumour. They wrap these things up in long words so that you don't quite know. They talk of rationalisation or consolidation, but what it really means is that they are going to close down our jam factory, and send all the fruit to Worcester. The first thing I knew for certain was when the manager called me into his office and said, 'Mr Martello, you have probably heard that owing to rationalisation we are closing down this jam factory. I see from the books that you have been with us for seventeen years. I only wish that we could keep you, but I am afraid that a number of good men are going to be made redundant. We are giving all our old permanent staff three months' salary in lieu of notice, and we will give you a very good letter of recommendation.'

All those long words simply mean that you are out of a job.

As I bicycled home by the short cut past the rubbish dump I kept saying, 'You won't be coming this way after the end of this month.' I knew every bush on the path, the very place where you pass an old rusty scrap motor car,

where you can start to freewheel, but it was all going to stop. Somehow I was a bit scared. It's not easy for a coloured man. I had a good responsible job, in charge of weighing the fruit, but it's not a job that leads anywhere. I wondered what Sannie would say, and about the kids' schooling and the payments on the double bed.

But Sannie was pretty good. She said, 'You can't keep a good man down, Klaas, and you're a good man.'

The first day I was free I went all round the dorp, but there aren't many jobs in a place like ours. I tried everywhere, even the dairies, by that night. Next day I couldn't think of anything to do, so I spent the day fixing the fowl hok, then in the evening I went to the bar for a brandy, and there I saw old Kosie. I suppose he had been there all day.

'It's not going to be easy for us. I just wish I was white, real white, then I'd show them,' he said.

I had my tot, and I was going home thinking about it all, and when I arrived, who should be having coffee with Sannie but Gertie Meyer. She's my wife's stepsister or something. There's a smart girl, but she never stops talking. She worked as a dressmaker at first, but when she found the money was better she changed to a hairdresser. As I came in she was saying, 'It's not only Cape Town; it's spread as far as America. Mrs Kennedy wears them. Of course they're expensive. Men as well as women buy them. When a man is getting a bit bald and he wants to impress a young girl, money is no object. I'm paid for every one I make up. It's not easy matching the hair, and fitting it properly, but I've been very successful. I've been making so much money that I'm thinking of buying me a motor car. For years the girls hanging around the docks have been wearing wigs, but now good-class coloured ladies are wearing them too.'

She stopped talking for one second to drink her coffee, and Sannie had a chance to say how they had closed the jam factory, and how I was out of a job. We walked down with Gertie to the bus stop, and I told them how Kosie had said, 'If only we looked real white.'

'There you are, Sannie!' Gertie said. 'If only Klasie had a wig to cover that crinkly hair.' Then the bus came in, and she had to climb on board. She was still leaning out of the window and talking as the bus pulled away. 'I reckon if Klasie got a wig he could even get a job as Prime Minister,' were her last words.

The next week I went down to Paarl and tried down there, but there were only a few temporary jobs picking fruit, but that is not the kind of work for a man who has been in charge of the scales at a jam factory. I couldn't accept it.

I was feeling very down when I came home, and Sannie seemed to be anxious when she asked me how I'd got on. 'Niks,' I said.

'Never mind. I knew you'd be hungry, so I've made kop-en-pootjies for dinner, and there is a parcel for you too.'

'A parcel? Who can have sent me a parcel?' Sannie acted all innocent but I could tell that she knew something about it. Even the kids crowded around as I opened it. It was a wig from Gertie, with a note which read: 'It won't sit down nice unless you shave all your own hair off.'

Sannie found the looking-glass and a pair of scissors, and in a few minutes my own hair was off and the new wig was on. It was beautiful, black, sleek hair, real upper class. I hardly recognised myself when I had it on. We had to chase the kids off to bed, they just wanted to sit around and stare at their own father.

Sannie and I stayed up late talking about the jobs I could apply for now. I know you might ask how a wig could make so much difference, but there are a lot of us good-class coloureds who look a bit white, and a lot of whites who look a bit coloured, so that it only takes a little change to move us from one group to the other.

Sannie had another bit of news, too. The porter at the Masonic Hotel in the next dorp had been fired for stealing the brandy. Why didn't I start by going there? It was a good-class job, with a smart uniform, and a peaked hat with gold on it, and it meant driving the hotel bus to the station.

So next morning I put my best clothes on and went there first thing, with my new hair neatly brushed. The old proprietor, Mr Goldman, read my reference from the jam factory. 'Mr Martello, I can see from this that you are a good, reliable man, and you would have been the man for the job, but for one thing. A lot of my business here is in the coloured bar, and sometimes you would have to stop quarrels and throw out drunks. I have been in the hotel business for forty years, and I know that job can't be done by a white man. The coloured people don't feel at home with a white man. They would go somewhere else. Another thing, if a white man gets drunk he feels ashamed if he has to be driven home by another white man, but it's all right if it is a coloured. I am sorry that you have had to call for nothing, Mr Martello.'

I was so shaken that I couldn't say a word, but as I turned to go I suddenly had an idea. 'Mr Goldman,' I said, 'I know I could suit you; I need this job. I have a sister-in-law who makes wigs. If I had a wig with crinkly hair, I'd look exactly like a coloured man. I know I would!'

The old man didn't look convinced. 'Well, it will have to look pretty good. These chaps aren't easily fooled, but I'll give you a chance. If you come back in a couple of days looking right, the job is yours.'

I left and hurried down to Gertie's place. 'Gertie, I say, can you make me a wig with crinkly hair?'

'What's the matter? Won't the dog let you into the house? We've had that trouble before.' So I had to tell her all about the job and Mr Goldman. Gertie is very quick. By the time she had stopped laughing, she had it all worked out. 'Klaas,' she said, 'come back in two days' time and I'll have you looking like a real Hottentot.' I didn't think that was very polite, but she meant well.

I came back when she said, and it was ready. I must say I felt more at home in it. When I went back to see Mr Goldman, he took a very long look at me. Then he said, 'Now you look just right, just the kind of coloured man I want. You will keep the place quiet and not frighten the customers away.'

It was a good job, too, with a lot of responsibility. I had to take the empties to the station and buy the vegetables at the market. And if any of the regulars had had a bit too much, I had to drive them home. It was the kind of job where a man was respected. People said, 'Good morning' to me now, people who hadn't even noticed me before, even some white people.

Mr Goldman helped me a lot, too, for he was a wise old man. He said one day, 'Don't be ashamed of being a servant. Everyone in the hotel is a servant; the purpose of a hotel is to give service. Be a proud servant. Proud of your service. The only measure of a man's true worth is the service he gives – from a king to a fruit-picker.'

Another day he said, 'People have often looked down on us Jews, but we don't care. We can hold our heads up high, because we know that we are good, for we are God's people. You must hold your head up high.' But it is sometimes hard for us coloured people.

It was through taking people home that I had my first rise. It was a young chap who had had a drop too much after a rugby game, and he turned out to be the son of the most important man in town, the president of the Fruitgrowers' Association. He and his wife were so glad to get their son back safe that he said that he would do anything that he could for me. So I asked him if he could fix to have the Fruitgrowers' Annual Dance at the Masonic this year, for I knew that was what Mr Goldman wanted more than anything else in the world. He was bitter that the Grand always got it, when we have the better room for dancing. He said he would try to fix it, and a few days later he came round and saw Mr Goldman.

That night, after closing time, the Goldmans were having their usual small brandy together when he called me in.

'Klaas,' he said, 'that was a smart move of yours. You've done the old Masonic a lot of good, and I'm going to give you a rise.'

'Yes,' Mrs Goldman said, 'we reckon we have one of the smartest coloured porters in the whole of Western Province.'

'But that's the big joke. He isn't really a coloured man at all! Show her, Klaas, how that's a wig you are wearing.'

'No, Mr Goldman, I don't wear a wig any more. My own hair has grown again.' And I gave it a tug to show him. He looked at me with his mouth hanging open for some time, every now and then giving his own hair a tug to see if it was tight on.

'But I remember when you first came here . . .' He shook his head. 'You've got me really puzzled. Ag, but what does it matter? It's a man's heart that counts, not his hair. Come on, have another drink.'

And that's a nice thing to say to a coloured man.

The Visitor

DEENA PADAYACHEE   1990

> Deena Padayachee grew up in Umhlali, practises medicine in Durban and is an Indian writer. In this slightly strange and disturbing story, he reminds us that it was in South Africa that Gandhi, later to be so prominent in the fight for the liberation of India from British rule, first developed his techniques of passive resistance. The tale conveys a satisfying mixture of peace and violence in its few pages.

It certainly was a free-for-all! Everybody was there – the little schoolboys who hadn't been to school for months, even old Phineas whose gnarled fingers were digging among the rubble for whatever he could find. Everybody!

And certainly the events of those sunny August days will stay with us for ever. For that one strange week it seemed as if all the constraints of civilisation had simply evaporated in Inanda. The rich – the shopkeepers, the landowners, the doctors – had fled, and we, the unemployed, the poor and the starving, could just walk into other people's homes and shops and help ourselves. We didn't need a second invitation. We climbed in!

Like so many people, I had been unemployed for more than a year when the events of that week unfolded; and this was despite my 'education', so that time came as a blessing for my fellow sufferers and me. I had even scavenged at the municipal rubbish dump in Kennedy Road which is in the Indian group area of Clare Estate. And more than once I had been involved in a bit of 'liberating' that had helped fill my belly. Being unemployed is a terribly frustrating business; your education becomes a mocking thing, accentuating your condition and making you feel even more useless. Actually I had mostly educated myself – many of our teachers were a bit of a joke and the syllabuses were often irrelevant and ridiculous. But luckily I love reading and I would get books from wherever I could.

The will to live is strong, and we did what we had to do. I was glad that my people were not becoming extinct like some Red Indian tribes.

On the Friday, the fourth day of pillage, I went along to the picturesque old Ashram nestling among some ancient Banyan trees on a small hill. During the previous night, the people had spoken of starting on it the next day. It was called the Phoenix Ashram and contained a health clinic which provided free medical care, a museum, a primary school and some old wood-and-iron homes. Some of the people spoke of a wise man who had once lived there called 'Gandhi'. Most of the people had no idea who he had been and what he had done in his life. Of course we had not learnt about him at school. I had read about him now and again in the newspapers, but at that time I knew very little about him.

The Ashram had a few people who looked after the place, but it attracted very important-looking visitors from all over the world. Or so young Zama who worked there had said. Anyway, that August day nobody was trying to look after the place; and Zama was just as energetically helping himself to what he could as anybody else was. Absolute mayhem reigned among the lovely old buildings. The noise of doors being ripped off their hinges and windows being shattered reverberated above a continuous cacophony of excited, shouting voices. However, I noticed that the people had not broken into the medical clinic. I ran into an old home and began taking what I could. I felt like a Goth stripping a venerable Roman lady of her garments. It felt good!

'This is better than the Group Areas Act,' I mused aloud to myself, thinking of the millions of people who had lost their homes because their race had made it illegal for them to live where they were according to this decree of the whites.

A crackly, piercing voice rose above the turmoil and proclaimed, 'Yes, at least this way the poor benefit.'

I turned and saw an old man standing in a corner of the dusty, shattered room. I had never seen him before. His horn-rimmed spectacles, skinny body and bald pate made him look rather vulnerable. How was he going to protect his loot from the others? And there was quite a mean bunch among the citizens who were working so hard that August Friday. I nodded and went outside with a box of stuff.

My friends were having the time of their lives. Tall Phineas, the boxer, was carrying off a large wooden window-frame on his head. Gladys, who worked as an ironing lady for some whites, was taking away a whole load of goodies on a rickety wheelbarrow. In the distance at the border of the riot-torn area, I saw army and police vehicles with their crews standing idly by. They had been spending taxpayers' money like that for a few days now; but they had made no attempt to intervene, thank goodness. I carefully selected a spot for my stuff and went back into the rapidly disintegrating house. The old man was peering anxiously at a delicate, faded, white blouse as I came in. It looked just the right size for a large doll. He held it up to the light, seemingly oblivious of the chaos around him.

Another loony, I thought, as I grabbed an old desk and began dragging the thing out. 'This is great,' I observed to the old man, 'being free with other people's enterprises. Maybe this is what the whites mean by the free enterprise system?' He turned then and looked at me; I swear that behind his toothy, insane grin there was, for an instant, a weary sad look of infinite pain.

'It certainly looks that way,' he said, and came over to help me with the desk.

'Thanks,' I said, wondering how much of *my* stuff he would want. He was strong; I'll say that much for him. As strong as a bloody ox. We had that desk outside in no time.

A cheer rose from the roof. Some of the corrugated-iron sheets were finally giving way. Carefully, Pieter and Petrus began lowering the iron from the roof. The old man was running his leathery fingers over the ancient desk slowly, like a man will slowly savour his wife's soft neck for the millionth time. He opened the desk and I saw his eyes come alive as he removed a book from inside. He began flipping the pages and paused now and again to read. I went over to look at the book. The cover said, *M K Gandhi, An Autobiography*.

'You're wasting time, old man,' I told him and dived back into the inferno. Eleven am on 16 August 1985 at the Phoenix Ashram outside Durban, South Africa, was just not the time or the place for reading.

'I'm leaving,' he said, and I turned quickly to look at him. I mean it was not as if the police or the army had suddenly decided to earn their pay or something. And he didn't seem to have taken anything yet.

There was that weird look in his eyes again. Was it just his strange spectacles? The kind of look that speaks of too much wisdom, too much understanding, too much love. He didn't have a shirt on and the white cloth wrapped crazily around his thin body was ragged.

'Yay! Old man,' I called, 'there's lots more loot in here; why don't you come in?' With his strong arms I would be able to liberate many more things in this place. His lean, dark hand was moving slowly over the desk as he gazed at the old home whose walls were coming crashing down. There was a kind of mist in his soft brown eyes, as they lingered over the splintered wood and the broken iron. 'No point in getting sentimental,' I said. 'In any case the people used to call that "The Empty House" because nobody lived there. It was a museum of some sort. At least now the people without homes will be making use of it.'

He smiled but there was no mirth in his eyes this time. 'That's true,' he said. Somehow the old man radiated an aura of dignity despite all the plundering that was going on around him. Inanda was in flames. He looked across the valley to where the police were, then at the desk. 'Look after these things,' he said in his gentle, squeaky voice, 'they are of Africa.' I thought that I detected a certain steel in his voice as he continued: 'Still the same old brainwashed puppets . . . puppets on a string, but someday their minds will not be alien to their souls . . . and then . . .' Resignation clothed his face but I thought his eyes still held a certain fire. He looked quietly at me. But he didn't finish the sentence. Instead, with a nod of goodbye he turned on his heel and moved off with long, marching strides on his sandalled feet. He didn't appear to really need the long staff he was carrying. And he hadn't taken anything from the Ashram.

There had always been a kind of unearthly peace in that old Ashram. A kind of freshness, a crispness of the air that left you exhilarated. The peace seemed to suffuse you and calm you no matter what the turmoil in your soul. Till that day when we looted the place. And somehow when that old man turned on his heel and strode off from the Ashram, all the peace in the place seemed to leave with him. I didn't feel like stealing after that. In fact I felt quite miserable.

But I kept the old desk. And at times when I look long and hard at it, I think I can see the old man's face looking up at me, and his eyes seem bright with life.

Some Other Elsewhere

MERLE COLBORNE   1990

Merle Colborne is one of the many South African writers who has moved away from her native country and now writes from abroad, in her case from County Mayo in Ireland. She was, however, born in the Cape and began her writing in Afrikaans. This story tells us something of the making of the Afrikaners, equating them with their 'Irish counterparts'. It is the writing of an exile, aware of and combining together very different worlds.

All her life she would remember the feeling she had then of not belonging. She had stood outside the living-room, staring at the torn frill of her dress, listening, not wanting to hear. And then she had tiptoed down the interminable passage towards the door, open on green hills nudging a damp sky. And she had run. Already the smell of turf and bog myrtle and the small manageable proportions made for weeping, the way a future empathy with brittle sunshine and the cavernous veld would one day make for weeping too.

Later she would attribute her strangeness to the migrations of her childhood and it was only in after years that she remembered, before ever having seen Africa, feeling a nostalgia for things she had never known. It was a feeling that had settled on her like a thin wrap of sadness, particularly when she was on her swing to- and fro-ing towards and away from the setting sun. As she tucked her calves up against the seat Mary saw, through her billowing dress, the geometry of the barn overlaid on a white-thorn kraal and the row of wind-break trees that knuckled up the hillside dissolving into bitter-leaved sisal. And as she stretched her legs into the air, she saw through her eyelashes, the sun, settling into its cloud-nest, transformed into a bloodied carcass savaged by the sudden fall of night in some strange elsewhere. And in the low moan of the milk cows coming home, she heard the bark of mountain baboon.

As the evening gentled into night, the kitchen door would open and her mother, silhouetted there against the bright rectangular postcard of light, would call that supper was ready. The smell of warm gravy and potatoes furled about her like a welcoming flag.

Her father often spoke of home, of Africa: of black women with petroleum jelly on their shins, who sat on the ground with their legs stretched straight out in front of them, talking with a clatter of tongues; of the black men who had worked for him, their teasing relationship which did not alter the respect they had for each other's strengths – and savageries.

Once her father had seen such a man across a damp Irish street and had dashed over to greet him with an elaborate handshake, an extravagant embrace. For her father missed black people and this man, though a stranger, being African, understood: the way (it later occurred to her mother) a Catholic and a Protestant might 6,000 miles and several years out of Belfast.

As an Afrikaner her father had a lot in common with his Irish counterparts. Both people had struggled against the British, both had fought to preserve a culture, a language and a literature. Sometimes, even, her father's imagination, seeing a rumpled Irish jaw jutting over a concertina at a ceilidh, cut to the face of an Afrikaner making boeremusiek.

But despite the similarities he found he could not come to terms with these maiden-voiced men who knotted handkerchiefs on their heads when the sun was barely warm, who prayed to an innocent girl in a blue sari for forgiveness for their sexual transgressions, who stood in their overcoats in the rain and talked interminably of draining boggy bits of land pegged out amongst the stones like old floor cloths vainly set to dry. And he could no longer abide the feeling – self-generated though it may have been – of standing constantly accused of everything his country's government had ever done. While he was guilty for having stayed there he was equally guilty for having left. His guilt was genetic, it came along with his colour.

And so, since it was again that time of year when the swallows lined the wires for the long southward flight, it should not have come as a surprise to Mary, to hear her father say those words: 'We're booked . . . home . . . Africa.' The words which had so confused her, had an immediate effect on her mother. They seemed to cause an implosion of her spirit so that she began to rue for everything that was still about her. She no longer lived in the present but in some imminent future where she would miss the past continuously.

And so they came to Africa. To her father it was, of course, coming home. He bought a house in a small town ('less lonely for you than out in the bundu,' he'd said) and a massive farm that he worked conscientiously. He was happy to be once again amongst sunburnt farmers whose foreheads were wrinkled from staring into a distant horizon, whose voices were as rough as the soil they strode, who did battle with a tough God.

In a strange way for her mother too, coming to Africa was in a sense a homecoming, a coming home of the psyche. For there was in her Irish soul, a comforting familiarity with the state of exile; homesickness was almost second nature to the Irish, part of their destiny. And Mother Ireland was never so much loved as when she loved from a distance . . . where her damp kisses and her strange possessive love that left no energy for other passions sat more lightly on her soul. Of course, she wept constantly.

'No fear of drought if you carry on like this,' her father quipped. But she just lifted misty eyes and, on St Patrick's Day, when others might wear green and tell Irish jokes, her mother wore black and prayed incessantly.

Mary started school and her mother made acquaintances amongst the mutton-armed women who lived in the small town. Since these were ladies who saw themselves as the epitome of moral rectitude she was surprised not so much by their politics (she was prepared for that) but by their attitudes to private things: they attached no guilt to contraception, no shame to divorce yet were shocked to hear that in Ireland she always kept a bottle of whiskey handy . . . in case the priest called.

Her mother found that she was tailor-made for maids. She had never been a very good housekeeper. There was always something tentative about the way she went about things, as though she were just filling in until someone far more capable would come bustling by, sleeves rolled up for the attack. Now she so much enjoyed coming into a room she had the previous night left bearing the signs of company – indented cushions, empty cups, full ash-trays – and finding it fluffed up and fresh-smelling. The minor rearrangement of ornaments that accompanied this pleasure was, to her, simply her signature on a document compiled by someone else. She did it with a flourish and a feeling of importance.

But she often felt sad. She missed her family, her acquaintants, the holy statues, the sign of the cross, the "grand day now!" greeting and most of all she missed the soft, atomising Irish mist. For in Africa she found the plump drops of rain that occasionally clattered into the dust turning the dongas into rivers the colour of bush-tea, too energetic for her.

Seeing the love her mother had for the land of her birth, the stubborn patria of her father, Mary developed a strange dichotomy of soul. She learnt – too young perhaps – that the prettiest flower is often poisonous and the plumpest portions of happiness usually contain a kernel of sorrow. She loved the stretch of her new country, the miles of mealie-land that cast a lattice of shadow on the red soil, the height and breadth of a sky so thick with blueness she wanted to tumble about in it. But she longed sometimes for a keen spring morning when dewy spider webs hung on the hedgerows like hammocks, for a brisk wind blowing in from the Atlantic. She sensed a change in her mother's love for her.

Mixed in with the natural and strongly physical love a mother has for a child, there was a new intensity, for when her mother held her, she felt too that she was holding a part of Ireland. And the joy she felt on seeing her (even after a short absence) called for instant expression: she needed to feel immediately the small diptych of her shoulder wings, the rococo curve of her back. And at night she kissed her fingers and, like a blessing, placed them on the small forehead.

And when mother and daughter strolled along the Main Road picking armfuls of cosmos, they spoke of the old boreen where, in summer, they had gathered meadowsweet and purple loosestrife, columbine and foxgloves, and, in autumn, blackberries by the bucketful and they spoke of the weather.

Mary sometimes thought that the quality of the climate summed up the difference in the characters of her two parents. And yet there was between them a deep attraction . . . as there is perhaps between the desert and a sky full of moisture. Sometimes, especially on Saturday afternoons, she felt wafting through the house, the quiet pleasure of their private sensuality. And then at tea-time her mother would look particularly beautiful . . . her amethyst eyes deeply set in dark, velvety lids shone like jewels of great value and the strong outline of her father's khaki-clad body seemed edged in a strange incandescent light. And there was a flowing together of their movements so that even the way her mother placed her finger on the knob of the teapot lid and the sure manner in which her father passed the biscuits, seemed to indicate a profound harmony.

But as time went on, her mother's sadness deepened and then developed into depression which seeped into her like dampness. Her father's way of coping was to walk around whistling hymns.

Her mother began to neglect the house; she lost interest in supervising, the maids in executing. Since she no longer gave praise, they no longer gave cause for it. Her mother spent much of her time locked away in her bedroom writing letters and sometimes when her father came in late from the farm, the songs he sang smelt of liquor and didn't sound at all like hymns.

In time her mother of course became ill as she herself had predicted. Doctors couldn't define it except to say that it was some sort of melancholia, an endogenous depression. She no longer wrote letters, no longer did anything at all.

Mary coped with her mother's illness as best she could. Because she wanted to be strong and brave – because she *was* strong and brave – she did not allow herself to ferret below the bravery and give expression to the darker feelings that naturally must have lurked there, and so the bewilderment, the sense of loss, the disappointment were not allowed to find the air and be dissipated. She buried all that so deep within her that she imagined it did not exist. And so life became something to be faced rather than to absorb or be absorbed by. Her mother, too, she handled in the same way as something that had to be dealt with – with kindness certainly – but also with control and so no real emotional involvement. *That* she kept for books and movies and small items in the newspaper – and then she wept with disproportionate grief.

Mary's mother now seemed to spend most of her time looking out of the window.

'What do you see?' Mary would occasionally ask but the dull eyes that slowly turned on her were answer enough. For though out there the washing, barely hung, was nearly dry, though slivers of heat peeled off the tin roof of the garage, though the fruit hung like huge goitres on the neck of the papaw tree, her mother saw: frozen linen on a frozen line, the pock-marked stalks of brussel sprouts and the shed door open on a cross-section of cut turf, like brown hexagons in a patchwork quilt of promised warmth.

And when she spoke, she spoke of funerals. She wanted to be buried, she said, not in some stony grave pick-axed out of a yellow unyielding earth, watched over by a few dusty cypresses and dishevelled bluegum trees, but upon a little hillock where the wind wound among the Celtic crosses and blew through the ruined church windows and the bare feet of a thousand monks shuffled over the ancient graves.

She did return, once, to Ireland. And there she talked often of Africa: of the fine drying weather, of black people and abundant fruit. And when she returned she found, for loving elsewhere a little less, she loved Africa a little more. But she would never again be entirely happy anywhere.

And so Mary learnt, not consciously, but effectively, to "set not her store by earthly things" or the soil on which she stood. And so a curious detachment, a strange individuality was born, that helped her to take all the permutations of fortune, suffer them, experience them and yet remain strong and true. Occasionally joy sprang up from a profound depth and percolated up through her whole being.

And so she learnt to carry her country within her and bear the loneliness of the crowd.

The Moment Before the Gun Went Off

NADINE GORDIMER 1991

Nadine Gordimer, who was born in Springs in 1923, was the winner of the 1991 Nobel Prize for Literature and the first South African winner of the award. She was born of a privileged White background which her works have consistently criticised. In its surprising ending this story from her recent volume, *Jump and Other Stories*, echoes something of the irony of Bosman with which this collection began, even though its tone is very different. As in so many of her stories she reminds us here of the central importance of personal relationships even within the political landscape with which she also deals.

Marais Van der Vyver shot one of his farm labourers, dead. An accident, there are accidents with guns every day of the week – children playing a fatal game with a father's revolver in the cities where guns are domestic objects, nowadays, hunting mishaps like this one, in the country – but these won't be reported all over the world. Van der Vyver knows his will be. He knows that the story of the Afrikaner farmer – regional Party leader and Commandant of the local security commando – shooting a black man who worked for him will fit exactly *their* version of South Africa, it's made for them. They'll be able to use it in their boycott and divestment campaigns, it'll be another piece of evidence in their truth about the country. The papers at home will quote the story as it has appeared in the overseas press, and in the back-and-forth he and the black man will become those crudely drawn figures on anti-apartheid banners, units in statistics of white brutality against the blacks quoted at the United Nations – he, whom they will gleefully be able to call 'a leading member' of the ruling Party.

People in the farming community understand how he must feel. Bad enough to have killed a man, without helping the Party's, the government's, the country's enemies, as well. They see the truth of that. They know, reading the Sunday papers, that when Van der Vyver is quoted saying he is "terribly shocked", he will "look after the wife and children", none of those Americans and English, and none of those people at home who want to destroy the white man's power, will believe him. And how they will sneer

when he even says of the farm boy (according to one paper, if you can trust any of those reporters), "He was my friend, I always took him hunting with me." Those city and overseas people don't know it's true: farmers usually have one particular black boy they like to take along with them in the lands; you could call it a kind of friend, yes, friends are not only your own white people, like yourself, you take into your house, pray with in church and work with on the Party committee. But how can those others know that? They don't want to know it. They think all blacks are like the big-mouth agitators in town. And Van der Vyver's face, in the photographs, strangely opened by distress – everyone in the district remembers Marais Van der Vyver as a little boy who would go away and hide himself if he caught you smiling at him, and everyone knows him now as a man who hides any change of expression round his mouth behind a thick, soft moustache, and in his eyes by always looking at some object in hand, leaf of a crop fingered, pen or stone picked up, while concentrating on what he is saying, or while listening to you. It just goes to show what shock can do; when you look at the newspaper photographs you feel like apologising, as if you had stared in on some room where you should not be.

There will be an inquiry; there had better be, to stop the assumption of yet another case of brutality against farm workers, although there's nothing in doubt – an accident, and all the facts fully admitted by Van der Vyver. He made a statement when he arrived at the police station with the dead man in his bakkie. Captain Beetge knows him well, of course; he gave him brandy. He was shaking, this big, calm, clever son of Willem Van der Vyver, who inherited the old man's best farm. The black was stone dead, nothing to be done for him. Beetge will not tell anyone that after the brandy Van der Vyver wept. He sobbed, snot running onto his hands, like a dirty kid. The Captain was ashamed, for him, and walked out to give him a chance to recover himself.

Marais Van der Vyver left his house at three in the afternoon to cull a buck from the family of kudu he protects in the bush areas of his farm. He is interested in wildlife and sees it as the farmers' sacred duty to raise game as well as cattle. As usual, he called at his shed workshop to pick up Lucas, a 20-year-old farm-hand who had shown mechanical aptitude and whom Van der Vyver himself had taught to maintain tractors and other farm machinery. He hooted, and Lucas followed the familiar routine, jumping onto the back of the truck. He liked to travel standing up there, spotting game before his employer did. He would lean forward, braced against the cab below him.

Van der Vyver had a rifle and .300 ammunition beside him in the cab. The rifle was one of his father's because his own was at the gunsmith's in town. Since his father died (Beetge's sergeant wrote "passed on") no one had used the rifle and so when he took it from a cupboard he was sure it was not loaded. His father had never allowed a loaded gun in the house; he himself had been taught since childhood never to ride with a loaded weapon in a vehicle. But this gun was loaded. On a dirt track, Lucas thumped his fist on the cab roof three times to signal: look left. Having seen the white-ripple-marked flank of a kudu, and its fine horns raking through disguising bush, Van der Vyver drove rather fast over a pot-hole. The jolt fired the rifle. Upright, it was pointing straight through the cab roof at the head of Lucas. The bullet pierced the roof and entered Lucas's brain by way of his throat.

That is the statement of what happened. Although a man of such standing in the district, Van der Vyver had to go through the ritual of swearing that it was the truth. It has gone on record, and will be there in the archive of the local police station as long as Van der Vyver lives, and beyond that, through the lives of his children, Magnus, Helena and Karel – unless things in the country get worse, the example of black mobs in the towns spreads to the rural areas and the place is burned down as many urban police stations have been. Because nothing the government can do will appease the agitators and the whites who encourage them. Nothing satisfies them, in the cities: blacks can sit and drink in white hotels, now, the Immorality Act has gone, blacks can sleep with whites . . . It's not even a crime any more.

Van der Vyver has a high barbed security fence round his farmhouse and garden which his wife, Alida, thinks spoils completely the effect of her artificial stream with its tree-ferns beneath the jacarandas. There is an aerial soaring like a flag-pole in the back yard. All his vehicles, including the truck in which the black man died, have aerials that swing their whips when the driver hits a pot-hole: they are part of the security system the farmers in the district maintain, each farm in touch with every other by radio, 24 hours out of 24. It has already happened that infiltrators from over the border have mined remote farm roads, killing white farmers and their families out on their own property for a Sunday picnic. The pot-hole could have set off a land-mine, and Van der Vyver might have died with his farm boy. When neighbours use the communications system to call up and say they are sorry about 'that business' with one of Van der Vyver's boys, there goes unsaid: it could have been worse.

It is obvious from the quality and fittings of the coffin that the farmer has provided money for the funeral. And an elaborate funeral means a great deal to blacks; look how they will deprive themselves of the little they have, in their lifetime, keeping up payments to a burial society so they won't go in boxwood to an unmarked grave. The young wife is pregnant (of course) and another little one, wearing red shoes several sizes too large, leans under her jutting belly. He is too young to understand what has happened, what he is witnessing that day, but neither whines nor plays about; he is solemn without knowing why. Blacks expose small children to everything, they don't protect them from the sight of fear and pain the way whites do theirs. It is the young wife who rolls her head and cries like a child, sobbing on the breast of this relative and that.

All present work for Van der Vyver or are the families of those who work; and in the weeding and harvest seasons, the women and children work for him, too, carried – wrapped in their blankets, on a truck, singing – at sunrise to the fields. The dead man's mother is a woman who can't be more than in her late thirties (they start bearing children at puberty) but she is heavily mature in a black dress between her own parents, who were already working for old Van der Vyver when Marais, like their daughter, was a child. The parents hold her as if she were a prisoner or a crazy woman to be restrained. But she says nothing, does nothing. She does not look up; she does not look at Van der Vyver, whose gun went off in the truck, she stares at the grave. Nothing will make her look up; there need be no fear that she will look up; at him. His wife, Alida, is beside him. To show the proper respect, as for any white funeral, she is wearing the navy-blue-and-cream hat she wears to church this summer. She is always supportive, although he doesn't seem to notice it; this coldness and reserve – his mother says he didn't mix well as a child – she accepts for herself but regrets that it has prevented him from being nominated, as he should be, to stand as the Party's parliamentary candidate for the district. He does not let her clothing, or that of anyone else gathered closely, make contact with him. He, too, stares at the grave. The dead man's mother and he stare at the grave in communication like that between the black man outside and the white man inside the cab the moment before the gun went off.

The moment before the gun went off was a moment of high excitement shared through the roof of the cab, as the bullet was to pass, between the young black man outside and the white farmer inside the vehicle. There were such moments, without explanation, between them, although often around the farm the farmer would pass the young man without returning a greeting, as if he did not recognise him. When the bullet went off what Van der Vyver saw was the kudu stumble in fright at the report and gallop away. Then he heard the thud behind him, and past the window saw the young man fall out of the vehicle. He was sure he had leapt up and toppled – in fright, like the buck. The farmer was almost laughing with relief, ready to tease, as he opened his door, it did not seem possible that a bullet passing through the roof could have done harm.

The young man did not laugh with him at his own fright. The farmer carried him in his arms, to the truck. He was sure, sure he could not be dead. But the young black man's blood was all over the farmer's clothes, soaking against his flesh as he drove.

How will they ever know, when they file newspaper clippings, evidence, proof, when they look at the photographs and see his face – guilty! guilty! they are right! – how will they know, when the police stations burn with all the evidence of what has happened now, and what the law made a crime in the past. How could they know that *they do not know*. Anything. The young black callously shot through the negligence of the white man was not the farmer's boy; he was his son.

Labour Pains

NORMAVENDA MATHIANE   1990

In accord with many of the other stories of the period, this simple fable tells of a new hope dawning in South Africa. It is placed here, slightly out of the usual chronological order, because it seems an appropriate ending to the collection as a whole. It looks forward with hope and expectation to a new world in the making. This new dawn results from the release in the year this story was written of Nelson Mandela, the leader of the African National Congress, after his many years on Robben Island, a prison for political prisoners off Cape Town. The immense impact of his release is discussed further in the general introduction to this collection. The 'Carter administration' refers to the period when Jimmy Carter was President of the United States of America.

As well as writing stories, Normavenda Mathiane is a journalist living in and writing about Soweto, a township just outside Johannesburg.

I got into the taxi and sat next to a pregnant woman, a picture of health. She sat there demurely displaying her happy and healthy state of well-being. For a moment I envied her contented appearance and wished her well.

The taxi went on collecting people. Soon it was full and on its way to town. I had forgotten about my neighbour when she nudged me and whispered, 'I am not feeling too well.' She moved slightly forward and balanced her hand on her hip. I closed the magazine I had been reading, and looked into her face. I don't know what I was looking for, but I didn't find it. I looked at my watch, the way midwives do. It was just after 7.30 am. I leaned toward her and asked her when she was due. She mumbled, 'Next month.' I asked her if it was her first baby she was carrying. She told me it was the second. We went on chatting about pregnancies and children and related matters.

Ten minutes later she grimaced and held on to her knee. I feared the worst was about to happen. I held her hand and told her not to worry, we would soon be in town and I would ask the driver to take her to the hospital. I also said she need not worry much, as it might be a false alarm. I felt good. I had used midwives' jargon. Clever.

Another pain struck. She held tightly on to my hand. I looked around and counted the women in the taxi – three. The rest were men, eight including the driver. She put her handbag on the floor and moved forward as if to give herself more room to breathe. Fanning herself with one hand and holding on to her knee with the other, she seemed to be in immense pain. I beckoned to one of the women and told her the problem. The man seated in front of me understood what was going on from our looks and exchanged seats with the woman whose help I was enlisting. No questions were asked as we sat watching the woman writhe in pain. Beads of sweat were running down her face. She no longer seemed to be conscious of her surroundings. The man next to us moved to give his seat to the other woman. The four of us sat there agonising. Someone told the driver what was happening and he reduced speed. All was quiet in the minibus. We were in the middle of nowhere.

Helplessly we watched cars drive past and wondered what we were going to do about the woman giving birth. We were now on the highway to town when the driver suddenly moved to the extreme left lane, crossed the yellow line and parked his vehicle. We transferred the woman to the back seat. One of the women started stroking the woman's belly while someone suggested we stop one of the passing cars and ask them to call for an ambulance. The driver got out to seek help.

Although the men would not look at what was going on in the back seat, anguish was written all over their faces. 'How far is she?' their faces seemed to ask, or 'Can't you make it easy for her?' We stood there knowing the effort was between her and the baby, and yet we were part of it. One of the women peeked between the woman's legs and said, 'She will be getting the baby in seconds now.' The woman was wailing silently and praying loud. Our nerves were about to snap. The woman kept rubbing her belly while some of us prayed.

Then she screamed. One of the older women took a peek and said, 'Come on now, my child, this is it – push.' The woman held on to our arms and started pushing. We were oblivious to the heavy traffic outside as we joined hands, minds and souls. I felt sweat come down my forehead and spine. I held tight to her hand as she clung to mine. She was sweating, grimacing and pushing with all her might when slowly the baby started appearing. It was like watching a movie, while at the same time being part of it, as the head gently broke out, made a turn and one by one the shoulders and wham! the legs were out. One of the women caught it, turned it upside-down and gave it a slap. The little thing released such a scream. We all started. And it was over.

I've thought of that morning, those many years ago, when the lives of so many strangers came to a standstill. I have thought of how the pain of birth, initially confined to the woman, had gradually engulfed the rest of us. I still carry the mental pictures of how we wrung our hands in desperate helplessness as she writhed in agony. We prayed with her and we suffered the pain with her.

Isn't it strange that none of us, as we got into the taxi preoccupied with the thought of our various destinations, had an inkling of what would befall us? How were we to know we would be part of a happening of such importance? Isn't it true that if we had been asked as we boarded the taxi if we wanted to share in such an experience we would have refused? But we did share in it. We were destined to experience the birth in that fashion and at that particular time.

Childbirth is unique with every woman. And every child has a route and manner different from other children. They may be born of the same woman but their circumstances are not the same. Some take days while others take minutes. Who dictates? It is a struggle and nobody can decide or dictate the form, shape or duration.

I have lived with the 'struggle' all my life – long before I could understand its meaning. I heard the struggle being pronounced by men at work. I have heard women mention the struggle as they carried on with their chores at home. To me, the struggle became synonymous with liberation. 'When the struggle is over . . .' I heard as a young girl when Jomo Kenyatta was fighting the British in Kenya. I heard it when Kwame Nkrumah led his people to independence in Ghana and I also heard it when he went into exile and there was talk of the country 'going to the dogs'. I was to hear it again at the Rivonia trial followed by the exodus of people leaving the country.

I have heard it many more times as I have grown older. At first it was not any of my business as one by one people in the struggle were detained or died. One mourned those one knew and hoped the whole nasty business could be sorted out. Gradually, like a net, people got dragged in. It was no longer Mandela or Sobukwe on Robben Island. 1976 came and went. Maybe it was the first pains. Perhaps the false alarm. The midwives looked at their watches, peeped and went back to the waiting rooms, continued knitting and reported the patient's progress simply as 'one finger dilated'.

They went on with their business: crocheting and knitting and talking about their families or discussing patients. Who cares? 'That woman in bed 5 is going to be here for days,' they said. But the woman in bed 5 was not just lying there and enjoying the comfort of the hospital bed. The moment for her to stop everything and begin the long process of delivery had come. It was just a matter of minutes before the nurses, the doctors, as well as people at home, would join her in the marvellous and painful task of bringing a life into the world. A matter of time.

During the Carter administration, a number of black congressmen visited South Africa. At an informal dinner held in their honour by one of the activists here, talk veered, of course, to South Africa's independence. Questions were thrown about and answered. Then one of the Americans, Congressman William Gray, asked, 'But are you blacks ready for it?' The question bordered on arrogance. Typical of all self-styled facilitators, he had given the situation a cursory peep and concluded the patient was far from delivery. But a Soweto leader, Mr Mosala, in his gentle and wise manner of talking saved the night. 'Does an expectant woman make an appointment with the baby to be born?' asked the man. While the woman may have a say insofar as conceiving, she has absolutely no say on how and when the child is to be born. How does one, therefore, say to a people, 'Now get ready, a new society is about to be born'?

A new society is not born by magic. It moves at its own pace. It determines the pace. It takes shape according to the specifics of its needs. For some countries the period was much shorter. Ours seems to take an eternity. Could it be the real pains or just a false alarm that we see the South African society disintegrate, and we watch our children become aliens to us, our culture and tradition? Whether it be false or real, the fact is that something to do with the new order is happening. A new society is being born and we are all sweating, writhing and pushing.

It begins humbly with individuals. Those who conceive of the idea, develop it. They get detained, skip the country, while the rest of mankind refuses even to talk about it. The architects continue while some fall by the wayside. And yet the seed already in the womb continues to grow. The individual tosses with the uncomfortable feeling of carrying. The rest of the people watch with apparent disinterest as the society changes. And soon, one by one, they begin to hold hands.

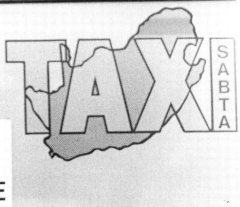

TAXI
D.I. MABASO
R325 GROUTVILLE
STANGER

A Note on Language

All the stories in this collection are in English. A few, mainly by Afrikaner writers, were written in their own language, Afrikaans, and then translated, generally by the author. It is important to remember that for White South Africans there are two official languages of equal status, Afrikaans and English. During the years of struggle, both the 'English' Whites and the African 'Blacks' tended to despise Afrikaans, as the language of the oppressor, but it will survive as a strong cultural influence, perhaps with something like the status of French in Canada.

Black writers tend to write primarily in English since this gives them access to a wider audience. Writing in tribal languages creates problems because of the linguistic differences between them, though there is still a strong and important tradition of oral story-telling.

Some of the words explained in the following glossary may be obvious enough to any South African reader. A typical example would be a word like 'braai', which is universally used to mean a barbecue in the same way as an Australian might refer to a 'barbie' or an American to a 'cook-out'.

As this example illustrates, where countries are in some ways similar to South Africa it is easier to find a more-or-less equivalent term. Thus one can find a good equivalent to 'veld' in Australian or Canadian English, such as 'bush' or 'prairie'; it is much more difficult to find one in British English, since there is no real geographical equivalent in the United Kingdom landscape.

South African English is a complex variety which combines words from many different cultures. In her editorial introduction to the Oxford University Press *Dictionary of South African English*, Jean Branford defines it as 'the English of South Africans of whatever race, colour, or national group . . . a lingua franca among those to whom English is, and many to whom English is not, their mother tongue. It teems therefore with words, ideas, structures and concepts from many languages and many cultures.'

This feature is well represented in the stories in this collection, where you will find words in Dutch, Afrikaans (itself a language of Dutch origin), numerous African languages, Irish, German and many other languages used alongside the more familiar words of standard British English. The glossary that follows attempts to explain the meaning of the less familiar words in the context of the stories in which they are found. Where a writer has used a few words from a Black tribal language in the story, these are generally translated into English immediately afterwards in the text so that difficulties here are minimal.

It is to be hoped that, as greater goodwill and exchange develop among the peoples of the new South Africa, we can expect to see the richness of their language and its vocabulary develop as well. One very interesting feature that is already happening in the bigger towns, such as Johannesburg, is the growth amongst young people of a new spoken language, based upon that of the 'tsotsis', but including elements from English, Afrikaans and other traditions. It may be that this, or something like it, will emerge as the common language of the future, although English is likely to remain the dominant written form, as in many other African countries where it has been adopted as an official language.

Glossary

Ashram	Indian religious place; a place of retreat where a religious community may be found
assegai	spear used by the Zulus made from the wood of the assegai tree, similar to mahogany, which was also used to make wagons
Baas	Master or Sir; the term usually used by non-Whites when speaking to a master or employer; meant to be a term of respect, but one that was very often used out of fear rather than real respectfulness. The new government actively discourages use of this word. (An Afrikaans word derived from the Dutch word 'baas' meaning 'captain')
Baba	father
bakkie	light truck with a cabin and open back used to carry people, animals or goods; a pick-up van
Bantu	general word used by many Whites to describe Africans; a term generally disliked by the Africans themselves, since it is not in any way accurate with regard to the wide variety of different tribes who make up the original African inhabitants of South Africa. The word originally meant simply 'people'
betel-nut	nut which is chewed to stain teeth red
Biko	Steve Biko, Black Consciousness leader killed while under police custody
bioscope	early word for cinema, still widely used in South Africa
blerry	'bloody'
boeremusiek	rhythmic country-style dance music, similar to American blue-grass music. The Afrikaans word 'boere' means 'country-style' as in 'boerewors', home-made sausages
boreen	a lane or narrow road in Ireland
bundu	wild, open country well away from cities and civilisation
burghers	citizens of the Transvaal and Orange Free State republics. (This usage derives from the Dutch word 'burgher' and originally meant a citizen of the Cape Colony who was

	not an employee of the Dutch East India Company and who was therefore a free citizen)
ceilidh	Celtic celebration usually in the form of a concert. This Gaelic word is still regularly used in Ireland and Scotland to mean a party at which music is played
Coloured	term usually applied to Black South Africans of mixed race, especially used of the Malay population of Cape Town known as 'Cape Coloureds'
commando	unit of specially trained mounted troops for hit-and-run raids in the Boer Army in the Boer Wars of 1888 and 1889 – 1902 (a word of Portuguese origin which has now passed into common international usage)
cosmos	garden plant with pink, white or purple flowers
cyclostyled	photocopied
dagga	cannabis, used as a slang term much in the same way as 'pot' or 'grass' (a word of Hottentot origin referring to a weed that grows naturally, especially in Natal)
dongas	a usually dry water-course running only at times of heavy rain (a word of Nguni origin)
dorp	country town or village; often used to refer to a backward place, a 'dump'. The Afrikaans word 'dorp' originally meant a village
ducoed	stained; coloured (used mainly for cars)
ehe	yes
fowl hok	chicken house (from Afrikaans 'hok', meaning a cage or pen)
Free State	abbreviated form of The Orange Free State, founded in 1836, to which the Boers migrated during their Great Trek when, under threat of political persecution by the English, they migrated from Cape Town in their ox-wagons
the Golden City	nickname for Johannesburg because of its association with gold-mining
half a crown	old unit of currency in Britain. A crown was worth a quarter of a British pound, so half a crown was one-eighth of a pound. The half-crown survived as a British currency unit until decimalisation, although the crown had disappeared a long time previously

Helele!	interjection of encouragement
Hottentot	one of the original inhabitants of South Africa at the time of the White settlement there; often used offensively. The word derives from an attempt by the Dutch to imitate the click-based language of the Xhosa people
jo-na-jo	expression of sorrow: 'poor me'
Kenyatta	Jomo Kenyatta fought for Kenya's independence and was its first president from 1964 until his death in 1978. He became one of the major leaders of post-colonial Africa
Kgele	interjection of astonishment
knobkerrie	club. Originally a Zulu and Xhosa fighting club, although the word itself is an Afrikaans one of Dutch origin
kop-en-pootjies	head and trotters, a stewed dish usually made of sheep's meat (from Afrikaans 'kop' (head) + 'en' (and) + 'poot' (foot))
koppie	a flat top or pointed hillock, a common feature in the South African landscape (an Afrikaans word derived from the Dutch)
kraal	enclosure for farm animals (a word of Dutch origin meaning the same as 'corral')
kroes	frizzy, curly [hair](Afrikaans)
kudu	African word for a large species of antelope with huge, branching horns
landdrost	the name for what was in the past the senior magistrate in a district; the word is derived from the Dutch words 'land' meaning country and 'drost', meaning a sheriff. The term is still found in 'the drosty (house)', the place where such a magistrate might live
a Letebele and a Russian	reference to two hostile groups, 'Russian' being the term used in Soweto for the South Sotho gangs which terrorised the townships from the 1940s onwards
lobolo certificate	marriage certificate. A word of Nguni origin, 'ukulobola', meaning to give a dowry. Therefore the word 'lobola' refers to the price traditionally paid, usually in cattle, by an African man to the parents of his bride
Ma-	female preface
Madam	the term of respect used by Black servants to refer to their

	female employers
matriculated	someone who has passed the 'Matric', the school-leaving examination required for university entrance: a widely used term not unlike the American use of the term 'graduation' from senior high school
mealie	maize; Indian corn (from the Afrikaans word 'mielie' meaning grain, especially millet)
merrum	Madam
mevrou	Mrs
mmate	friend, mate
mtombo	sprouted grain often used for brewing beer, especially home-brewed; very similar to malt
mule	as used here, a kind of rallying cry or war-cry
nooi	girl, girlfriend
1976	year of the Soweto Riots
16 August 1985	State of Emergency declared
niks	Afrikaans for 'nothing'
Nkrumah	the first president of independent Ghana (previously the Gold Coast) who was later deposed and died in exile in 1972
pass	passbook that all Africans had to carry as an identity document and which became a symbol of their oppression by the Whites
puma	large, wild member of the cat family
quirt	type of riding whip with a short handle and a braided leather lash about 2 feet long
the Rand	the old mining area around Johannesburg, also known as the Reef. The word derives from an Afrikaans word meaning a ridge overlooking a valley
rand note	the rand is the South African unit of currency
the Reef	the industrialised gold-mining area which centres upon Johannesburg
Rivonia trial	the trial in 1964 when Nelson Mandela and 10 others were charged with sabotage and attempting to overthrow the South African government. All except one were sentenced to life imprisonment and the 7 non-whites were taken to the prison of Robben Island

shebeen	a place where liquor is served illegally without a licence, usually by African women known as 'shebeen queens', as here. The word comes from the Irish and originally meant a bar where illegally distilled liquor was served
skollie	thug, gangster
Sobukwe	Robert Sobukwe, Pan African Congress leader
Standard Eight	Form III – third year of High School
stoep	raised platform around a house to provide a verandah for sitting on; the same word as the American and Canadian 'stoop'
Teyateyaneng	town in Lesotho
township	an area set aside under the Group Areas Act for non-White occupation by Blacks or Coloureds
umphako	food provisions for the journey
veld	a term generally applied to the natural South African countryside, very like the Australian use of 'bush' or the 'prairies' of Canada or the USA
wai	interjection expressing contempt